LIVING FREE SOLUTIONS

LIVING FREE SOLUTIONS

Cooking for the Gluten, Casein, Soy, and Yeast Free Home

Asian Cuisine
Collection

HUONG DISHIAN

TATE PUBLISHING
AND ENTERPRISES, LLC

Published by Tate Publishing & Enterprises, LLC
127 E. Trade Center Terrace | Mustang, Oklahoma 73064 USA
1.888.361.9473 | www.tatepublishing.com

Tate Publishing is committed to excellence in the publishing industry. The company reflects the philosophy established by the founders, based on Psalm 68:11,
"The Lord gave the word and great was the company of those who published it."

Published in the United States of America

ISBN: 978-1-62147-447-0
1. Cookbook
2. Special Diet
12.11.15

ACKNOWLEDGMENTS AND DEDICATION

I would like to thank God. His love and guidance has helped our family endure the peaks and valleys of life. He shown me a new side of me that I ignored for years—a love for cooking. He blessed me with strength I didn't know I had. My family and I would not be where we are today without his Grace.

I am so thankful to my husband, Jim. This process wasn't easy for him; it brought back the emotional roller coaster we went through. He put his feelings aside and helped wherever and whenever I needed him. I wouldn't have being able to do this without his love and support.

I have been blessed with two loving and talented moms. My mom, Tam Pho; cooking was her gift. She could create many recipes, successfully, on her first try. Everyone loved her cooking. When I was a teenager, she kept trying to teach me how to cook, and I would run away every single time. Then one day, she received a phone call from me asking for help with cooking. She came over immediately and was ready to teach me to cook Vietnamese foods. My mom passed away a little over two years ago. She will always be in our hearts. I am so glad that I was given a second chance to learn from her and that I am able to pass it on to my children. I truly would not be where I am today with cooking without her.

My mother-in-law, Peggy Dishian, is incredibly loving. There isn't anything she wouldn't do for her children, her in-laws, and her grandchildren. I am so grateful for her love and support. From the day we informed the family of our eating plan, there were never any strange looks or questions of why; it was simply, "How can I help?"

Peggy would travel any and all distances, going to specialty stores to make sure that the boys had food to eat at her house. It's such a relief for me not to have to pack food for the boys when visiting Grandma and Grandpa.

My two special boys, Johnny and Joshua, are my lights. They are such troopers and will try anything I put in front of them, good or bad. I can always count on them to give their honest opinion.

"It needs a little more work, Mom," Joshua, my Little Messy Chef, would say. He is a great kitchen helper, even at a very young age. He would give a lot of ideas on foods he wanted to try. Johnny is the total opposite. He is less messy in the kitchen and satisfied with whatever we're making. I am so grateful for the many wonderful and fun cooking adventures we have had together.

Thank you to all our friends and family members that have been there for us. Your interest and support have really helped us more than you know, especially on those bad days.

I would also like to dedicate this book to the readers—the parents and families with autistic and special needs children. I know how difficult it can be, changing to a new eating plan. You can do it! I've been in your shoes, and I know you can do the same for your family.

TABLE OF CONTENTS

Part 1: JJ Base and Premade Pantry Recipes

Part 2: Sauces

Part 3: Grab-n-Go

Part 4: Dinners

Photo Reference

Part 5: Sweet Treats…

Part 6: Bread

Part 7: Breakfast

Printables

BACKGROUND WITH AUTISM AND THE SPECIAL DIET

Over twelve years ago, we were faced with the news that our first child was diagnosed with autism disorder. At the time, this was a rare disorder, not well-known by many people including medical professionals. Now, however, autism is considered an epidemic, more common than Down syndrome. Sadly, a recent research shows that autism affects *1 in 88* children in the United States today. That's compared to 1 in every 5,000 in 1980. It is projected that in the United States alone, more than one million people suffer from autism.

Autism is a developmental disorder, appearing during the first few years of life. Autism affects the brain's normal development of communication and social learning. Some of the most common symptoms include difficulty developing nonverbal communication, delay or lack of speaking, repetitive use of language, difficulty understanding others, unusual focus on pieces, body rocking, hand flapping, or preoccupation with certain topics.

If you are concerned that your child may be modeling symptoms of autism, I encourage you to discuss your concerns with a professional autism specialist or your primary care doctor as soon as possible.

When our son was diagnosed, it took us two years to figure out what was wrong. Today, there are many resources and options available to help you and your family. Although it's not a guarantee, early intervention is extremely important in improving your child's chances.

WHAT IS AUTISM?

Autism is a neurological and biological disorder. Autism spectrum disorder and autism cover a broad spectrum of complex disorders of brain development. The disorders are depicted in various ways, such as difficulty in social interactions, communication (verbal and nonverbal), and rhythmic behaviors.

According to research, autism spectrum disorder begins in the early stages of brain development. The signs of autism are not obvious, however, until two to three years of age. The disorder affects individuals differently, with different degrees of severity.

There are many publications available that will provide more in-depth explanations associated with this disorder. Be sure to ask your child's specialist.

As you talk to a professional in this field, you're likely to hear about a recommended special diet (gluten-free, casein-free, and soy-free) as an intervention treatment.

Of all the interventions and treatments, the gluten-free, casein-free, soy-free (GFCFSF) diet is usually the most difficult because it is a complete *lifestyle* change.

WHY THE GLUTEN-FREE, CASEIN-FREE, SOY-FREE (GFCFSF) DIET?

Some studies showed that, ASD children have a difficult time digesting foods with gluten, casein, and soy protein. Because of the inability to digest these foods properly, ASD children tend to have more allergies as well as sleep problems. The latest scientific evidence indicates that digestion of gluten proteins (found in wheat, barley, rye, and grains) and casein (found in milk, cheese, and yogurt) is often a problem for autistic people. Foods with gluten, casein, and even soy can aggravate and intensify autistic symptoms. There is a belief that an autistic child's brain treats gluten, casein, and soy like a false opiate. The chemical reaction leads an autistic child to act in a certain way. By excluding these items from your child's diet, you can improve your child's digestion and other facets of their life.

IS IT NECESSARY TO ELIMINATE ALL THREE?

The answer is really up to you. In my son's case, we eliminated all three foods and yeast to give our son the best chance to succeed. The effects of the diet are hard to prove because it really depends on how individuals go about the diet. Below is a research posted on the TACA Now website:

> In 2002, Dr. Harumi Jyonouchi performed a study with autistic children. He changed their diet to a gluten-free/casein-free/soy-free diet. The research showed that 91% of children with ASD who were put on a strict GFCFSF diet, improved compared to the 65% improvement with just GFCF alone. Jyonouchi's study shows that ASD children have an abnormal immune response to the proteins in soy, gluten, and casein. By changing an autistic child's diet to that of gluten-free/casein-free/soy free, improvement will be seen. Countless parents reported that the diet was very beneficial for their child. The most common comment we hear from parents is that their child seemed to "come out of a haze."

This diet is not much different than other diets that each of us have tried at one point or another in our lives—you'll get out of it what you put in. Over twelve years ago, we didn't have any research statistics to go by and the idea of eliminating gluten was considered crazy. Our decision was made based on faith and determination to give our son the best life we can.

Today, gluten sensitivity is not just related to celiac disease and autism, there have been so many reports of health concerns linking to gluten, including chronic fatigue, depression, abdominal pains, constipation, or mood swings. Like any diet plan, be sure to consult your physician before you begin, to ensure healthy outcomes.

Once you've made a decision to try this diet for ASD or other health-related issues, my hope is this book will help you transition to this new lifestyle with ease. The cooking method and recipes can easily be changed whether you want to eliminate just gluten or all three.

OUR JOURNEY

Like many families, autism took us by surprise. Johnny was a healthy baby. There were no signs in his early development that anything might be amiss. He made great progress with his development. He spoke his first word at the age of ten months and walked before his first birthday. I even taught him a few Vietnamese words!

I'll never forget the week before his birthday; Johnny grabbed the birthday party invitations, ran, and laughed all the way to the family room. Little did I know that was the last laugh I would hear from Johnny for a very long time.

Shortly after his first birthday, Johnny's development started to go downhill. He started sleeping less, his communication slowly changed from talking to crying to screaming. His eye contact with others lessened as well. He would stay awake in his bed until two o'clock in the morning only to wake up at six o'clock, screaming. His hands were constantly flapping or jerking. I'll never forget the time we put a little CD player in his room to play soothing music, thinking it would help him sleep. We didn't hear any noise and thought it was working. Unfortunately, instead of helping him sleep, he was captivated by the turning of the digital numbers. He would stare at the digital numbers turning until the CD player stopped.

As each day went by, I saw that our son was slipping further away from us and deeper into another world. The bad news didn't stop there. Eventually, it got to the point that the slightest sounds bothered him. The sound of the windshield wipers made him scream; he hid in the closet at the sound of a baby's cries. His sense of touch was heightened and sensitive. I'll never forget the first time I took him to get a haircut. He screamed "Bloody!" loud and over and over as if it was killing him.

Christmastime was the worst for us. Like many parents, we bought him a lot of presents. We wanted, so much, for Johnny to have a good Christmas. Christmas morning, Johnny came down the stairs, saw the presents, and ran back upstairs. He ran away from any rituals or events that involved his participation. The warmth of the holiday's feelings was nonexistence for us.

My husband had numerous conversations with Johnny's doctor, and every time the response we got was there wasn't anything wrong. In regards to Johnny's sleep problems, the doctor said, "Every child needs a different amount of sleep!" We just couldn't accept that this was the case and there wasn't anything wrong. My husband and I spent countless hours researching and seeking answers.

By the age of two, Johnny rarely said a word. He didn't want to play with other kids, didn't like to be touched or hugged, and pretty much preferred to be left alone. He was a two-year-old with bags under his eyes. He communicated with us by screaming and didn't seem to notice much of his surroundings. We couldn't go anywhere without facing a tantrum or strange looks from people. Sunday mornings, we would be in church and then have to leave about five minutes after the service started because Johnny's assigned nursery number would flash on the screen. It was so bad, there were times I would see a mom dealing with children bickering with each other and I wished I had her problems.

My husband and I continued to keep seeking answers from our son's doctor. Every time we noticed a strange reaction, whether it was his behavior or something else, we would talk to the doctor. We continued to get the same answer: "Nothing is wrong." There were times I watched him staring into space. I just broke into tears wondering where he was. *Doesn't he know that we're here for him?* I'd think to myself, *Where did we go wrong?*

Many times I wanted to hug him so badly, but he would turn away, not liking to be touched. One year, we decided to enroll him in daycare, hoping it will help him be more socialized. There was a little girl that dragged Johnny around like a toy, and Johnny didn't even respond.

Labor Day 1999 is a weekend we will never forget. Our second child, Joshua, was about four months old. We needed to get away. Our options were limited given Johnny was not comfortable with changes and being around people. We decided to visit my brother's family who lived in a suburb outside of Chicago, Illinois. We experienced a pleasant surprise when Johnny went to sleep within minutes of tucking him in bed and didn't wake up until noon the next day.

We were in shock and couldn't believe that this was our child. My sister-in-law thought maybe the different environment helped him. Although this was a nice thought, we didn't believe it was the case. We continued to observe Johnny's behavior the whole weekend. We were ecstatic to see Johnny sleep more and being calmer the whole weekend but were very curious as to what was happening. On the way home, we stopped for lunch at a Burger King. Johnny climbed up on the "play tube" (he had never done this before) to the top and looked down at us. It was the first time we saw our happy little boy again after two years. Unfortunately, it didn't last long. Johnny was back in his sleepless routine that night.

We could not believe his behavior had taken such a turn within a few hours of being home. At this point, we were determined to figure out what had happened. We stayed up all night to write down every event, every food, drink, and behavior we observed that weekend. As it turned out, it was the milk. You see, Johnny refused to drink the milk my brother had at his house. There wasn't a grocery store nearby, and we didn't want to burden them. So Johnny didn't drink milk the whole weekend. We felt guilty on the way home and bought him milk. Little did we know what the milk was doing to his body. We eliminated the milk, and he started sleeping longer. I wish I could tell you that our problem was solved at this point.

We took an experimental step and eliminated casein from his diet. It was definitely a step in the right direction. With more sleep, he was a less irritable. His other behaviors and symptoms had not gone away. My husband and I spent countless hours researching and talking to people to find out as much as we could about food issues associated with behavior. We came across the idea of a hair analysis test to help us understand what was happening inside his body. We anticipated the results to show some type of nutrition imbalance. The results stunned us: his lead and mercury levels were off the charts.

We began to talk to many professionals, including a pediatric neurologist. They diagnosed him with autism. They told us there was no cure, nothing they could do for Johnny. The doctors suggested that we shouldn't have any more children. It was devastating news to us. It took us a little over two years to find out what was happening to Johnny. We weren't about to give up on our son now.

We started searching on the Internet, read many books, and sought out anything we could find on autism. We tried auditory integration therapy, detoxification/chelation, Nambudriead's allergy elimination technique, attended the relationship development intervention (RDI) seminar, and various therapies. We came across the *Biological Treatments for Autism and Pervasive Development Disorder (PDD)* book by Dr. William Shaw. This led us to the DAN organization and then to the GFCFSF recommended diet. The information here also mentioned the yeast infection and bacterial overgrowth problem in autistic children. We had Johnny take the organic acid test, and he showed positive fungal overgrowth in the intestinal tract. At that point, we also eliminated yeast from his food. Of everything we had tried, the results were nothing compared to the results we saw with the diet.

At that time, we found and read a lot of skeptical comments on the recommended diet theory. Many people commented that it didn't work for them. We thought the change of diet theory made a lot sense because it addressed the root-cause of the problem. We thought it was worth giving it a chance, regardless of the skepticism.

We've decided to remove gluten, casein, soy, and yeast from his diet. We figured why not go all the way and give Johnny's body the greatest possible chance to function the best it could? If we didn't, we would have always wondered, *What if?* because we didn't give it our all. *It turned out to be the best intervention with the most results.*

The chelation and detox-program flushed out the lead and mercury in his body. The enzymes for GFCFSF were used as a part of their supplements. This helps Johnny's body properly digest the proteins properly, just in case a trace of it got in, inadvertently.

After two years of frustration and feeling hopeless, the decision to go on the diet was easy. Like many that decide to do this diet, we were hyped up and ready to go. It didn't take very long before the reality hit that this diet eliminated 80-90 percent of the foods available at the grocery stores. Specialty shops were far and few, not to mention that the foods were expensive, even if you could find it.

Adding on top of the challenge of finding the appropriate foods, I wasn't much of a cook. I knew how to cook rice, make ramen noodles, and order carryout foods. Living over half of my life in America,

I wanted the American dream that I always heard about as a young girl in Vietnam. My plan was to have a great career and climb the corporate ladder. I dodged my mom every time she wanted to teach me how to cook because cooking wasn't in my plan; having a career was my focus. My plan was going great. I was a project lead by time I was twenty-three, leading an IT organization at age of twenty-seven. That was my plan, though, not necessarily *God's* plan. I was headed for a lot of challenges with the dietary requirements. Not only did I have to learn how to cook, I had to learn how to cook specialty foods that no one I knew could teach me.

I had to continue to work, but my career plan was pretty much on the backburner. My drive was turned from a corporate career to figuring out how to feed Johnny. The beginning was extremely difficult and frustrating. I spent most weekends from six o'clock in the morning until midnight, cooking. Unfortunately, about 80-90 percent of the food, especially bread, ended up in the trash can because they were like bricks and tasted like sand. I bought cookbooks and searched for recipes on the Internet. Most recipes were either GF, but not SF and CF, or YF, or vice versa. So the combination of eliminating all these ingredients in recipes was extremely difficult to find.

After several weeks of getting into it, I was exhausted and tired with barely enough for Johnny to eat. He was getting by with mostly rice, one of the few items I managed to make for him. I felt inadequate and like a failure. Like many parents, I wanted so much for my kids to have "normal" foods. You see, that was my mistake. Growing up over half of my life in America, normal food in my mind was bread, pizza, hamburger, and hot dogs. One late night while I was throwing away another batch of bread, I was extremely frustrated with myself for not being able to give my son a decent meal, again. Then, a little voice inside me yelled out, "You didn't eat very much bread or drink cow milk or any of this stuff growing up, dummy!"

It was like a lightning bolt just hit me. Most of my childhood foods consisted of rice, tapioca, or coconut milk, etc. The next day, I called my mom and to ask her to teach me how to cook Vietnamese foods. Finally, my mom had my attention with cooking. After learning the basics from my mom, I began to merge culinary ideas from both countries and began to create many of the recipes that not only helped my children feel that they are not missing out but also have unique foods like a hot pocket, Vietnamese style.

Several months went by, and we didn't see any significant changes. We knew going in that it was going to take a while before we saw improvements. Still, it didn't keep me from wondering: *Is this working? Am I wasting my time? Am I crazy to try this?*

Of course, the exhaustion didn't help. As you enter this lifestyle, it's likely that you'll be asking the same questions. I want you to know that this feeling is natural. It's okay to feel this way. I felt it, and many times I came very close to calling it quits, but I am glad I didn't. To really know for sure, one must be patience with this transition. It takes a child's body quite a while to flush all the gluten out, sometimes more than a year.

Six months went by; Johnny had just turned four. I was working long hours, using every moment of free time I had in the evening and weekends to make foods for Johnny. We hadn't seen any sign of changes with Johnny. He still wasn't talking much. His little brother, Joshua, was walking now. Joshua would constantly take Johnny's toys away from him, and Johnny never reacted to it or even noticed what his brother did. One afternoon, Johnny and Joshua were in the family room. I just finished making a batch of hot pockets. I leaned over the sink and felt numb. I broke into tears, staring at the water dripping from the faucet.

All kinds of conflicted emotions crossed my mind. I was feeling hopeless.

This is just too hard. I am exhausted, and he hasn't shown any sign of improvements!

I wanted to quit. I fought those feelings, refusing to give up on my son. Every time I wanted to quit, it took every gleam of hope I had to overcome the doubts and to get me going again. As a little girl, I saw my father's persistency and perseverance that saved us from a war that ended badly and got the family to America. Now, I am at the same crossroad for my son. The situation was different, but the struggles and the anxiety of the unknown outcome were the same.

I was so exhausted and could barely stand up. I asked God to give me strength. Then I heard a voice coming from the family room: "Give it back!"

I ran in the living room. Jim ran down from upstairs. It was Johnny responding to his brother for taking his toy. My tears could not stop pouring. From that moment on, we knew we had to make this work. There was no question in our minds that this was going to be the lifestyle for us moving forward.

It was time to find a solution to simplify our lives with this diet. Every time I cooked or purchased foods, I was constantly trying figure out what was really *necessary* and what was *nice to have*. Anything that created more work and added no value to our lives, I cut out.

For the next few months, we continued to see subtle changes in Johnny. His eye contact was focused on us a little longer than usual, and he started using gestures to communicate with us. Little by little, we started to see our little boy coming back to us.

Years later, the little subtle changes turned into big milestones. We started to receive compliments from his teachers about the differences they saw in Johnny. Through the years, he started to overcome academic challenges. His grades went from mostly *pass* and *fail* to C's, and slowly moving up. He made honor roll for the first time in his freshmen year!

Today, John is almost sixteen, a sophomore in high school. He likes basketball and ping-pong and loves to make friends. His teacher always comments on what a good student he is. We've recently received Johnny's state end-of-the-year assessment score. He achieved an advanced level on his math score. (It's not an autism thing. Math skill runs in our family.) He likes to be funny and has a good one-liner now and then. He's very proud of himself when people laugh at his jokes.

Besides the academic milestones, I noticed several other wonderful traits about Johnny: He is very kind and caring, always looking out for his brother. At his brother's birthday party, he wanted to use his own earned money to buy his brother a present. He's honest, always telling us the truth and what he thinks. He is passionate; he already wants to invent a memory machine and to have his own business someday. He doesn't give in to peer pressure. At social events, if someone gives him something he knows he shouldn't eat, he has no problem saying no. He doesn't have a need to prove himself to his peers. He is persistent and perseveres, whether it's seeking to understand something or having a lot of homework. He is very disciplined with getting his homework and chores done on time.

Johnny had his first sleepover last summer with his cousin, Michael, and a friend, Jalen. He had such a great time and asked me why he hadn't done this before. He wishes he had done this when he was younger. I couldn't help but to smile and hug him. These moments may not mean much for parents with children not on the spectrum. But they are golden to us.

As hard as the transition was, I could not imagine where Johnny would be today or what our lives would be like if we didn't give it our all. Given the growing success with many families, I believe we would still be wondering, *What if?*

My hope is that this book gives you hope and encouragement that you *can* make this happen no matter what your situation may be. The odds were against me from the start. I didn't know how to cook nor want to be a cook. If I can do this, so can you.

Don't let the fear of change keep you from giving this way of eating a chance to work. Although this lifestyle is a big change, it's not impossible. It was much harder not knowing and feeling helpless. I'm optimistic that this method and the recipes in this book will help you help your family make the transition more easily and quickly. I've compiled these recipes to be as user-friendly as possible. It's a blend of classic American favorites as well as dishes from my Vietnamese culture.

7 HABITS FOR A SUCCESSFUL START

It will take times to learn about the foods and nuances with purchasing and preparing foods. Following are the *7 Habits* that have greatly helped me, and I hope they will also help you ease through the transition successfully.

1. *Always read your food labels*. Learn about the ingredients allowed, not allowed, and hidden ingredients. The "Special Helpers" section in this book includes a list of foods and ingredients for the diet and a printout of guidelines that will give you a great start.

2. *Verify. Verify. Verify.* Before buying or eating. It's better to be safe than to regret it later. If you plan to eat out, call and verify the ingredients and food preparation with the restaurant's chef ahead of time. One of the rules of thumb I gave the boys in case they get a food item from school, "Don't eat it, and bring it home for us to verify first!"

3. *Stay true to the diet*. Don't treat this like a weight-loss diet that you can indulge and get back on. A "little bit" can set your child's progress back.

4. *Introduce* one *new food at a time*. This will help you isolate the problem. Listen to your body. What works for others does not necessarily work for you, or vice versa. If your child is too young, observe their behavior changes.

5. *Plan ahead*. Healthier foods come with higher costs. With a little planning once a week, you can stock up and save on your frequently used ingredients. Planning ahead will reduce your food preparation time too. This book includes many tips on making multiple meals with the recipes.

6. *Keep it simple*. Start out with basic-ingredient recipes. Choose recipes that are adult- and kid-friendly to make one type of meal for the family instead of two types. Once you are comfortable with making the basic items and your cooking plan, then use the extra time you have to try new ingredients or recipes. Trying to make too many items when you're new to the diet can be costly and will only create more frustration for you.

7. *Have a positive attitude*. Don't limit your thinking. Food can be delicious as well as safe and healthy. I taught my kids at a very young age, it's not that they can't have certain foods, their

food just needs to be prepared differently. There are many advantages in making your own food—saving money and more control with what goes into your food. For example, you can make it healthier by reducing the sugar content and use healthier fats such as olive oil, etc.

The "Special Helpers" section contains more detail on food lists, other helper tips, and other resources to help you on your way.

ABOUT OUR RECIPES AND METHOD

The first few things you'll notice on the diet is over 70 percent of food in your grocery store contains gluten, dairy, soy, or yeast. Additionally, buying premade foods for the diet or eating out can be pretty expensive.

After many trials and errors, I began to create my own method to simplify the cooking process, reduce food costs, and a plan that works with our busy lives.

Besides meats and vegetables, most foods are basically prepared with flours, bread crumbs, or sauces. So I began to create a "base" method for all these items. These base items can be made ahead in big batches and used in many recipes to shorten cooking time, waste less, and save money. Every time I want to try a new recipe, I always start with the base items first.

I came up with four types of base recipes: two base flour blends, a base crumbs, and a base sauce. This method really helped me with food planning, reduced grocery items, and gained back some "me time" and "family time." These base items are named with a *JJ* prefix to distinguish them in the recipes; plus the boys love the idea of having their initials on these items.

TWO BASE FLOUR BLENDS METHOD

Gluten-free baking requires multiple flours to work like wheat flour. There are many different gluten-free "all-purpose" flour mixes available for purchase. However, there are drawbacks and can be pretty expensive. Each brand has different taste and has different results on your recipes. It takes five minutes to make your own blend and less expensive.

The two base flour blends used in the recipes are:

- The *JJ Cake-Base Blend* is use for baked goods that have a fluffy, soft, or cakey texture, such as cakes, muffins, breads, pastries, etc.
- The *JJ Cookie-Base Blend* is used for baked goods that have a dense texture like cookies, brownies, etc.

These blends are made ahead and consist of the basic rice flour and starches for easier storage and conversion. In a recipe, the Base Blend is then used with another GF flour, such as brown rice flour, sorghum, or other GFSF flours. The second flour allows you to adjust the result to your preferences, such as higher fiber, different texture (chewy, cakey), etc. It also gives you a way to experiment as you get more comfortable with the diet and customize to your own preference. Most of the recipes in the book use brown rice or sorghum flour. I find that other bean flours leave an aftertaste and are not very kid-friendly.

BASE CRUMB METHOD

When it comes to a base crumb, I wanted to make it simple, crunchy, and good tasting.

- The *JJ Crumbs-Base Blend* is tasty and can be used with savory or dessert dishes.

BASE SAUCE METHOD

There are so many different sauces and ways to make them. Sauce with thin consistency is easier to prepare along with the dishes. The thicker sauce usually takes more time and more ingredients. To reduce time, I wanted to come up with a thick base sauce that can easily turn into many flavored sauces and marinades.

- The *JJ Sauce-Base* has a nice balance of sweet, tangy, and salty. This base sauce is used in either American or Asian recipes in this book.

These base recipes are in the "JJ Base and Premade Pantry Recipes" section of this book. In addition to these bases, the recipes in the book are made with ingredients that are free of gluten, casein, soy, and yeast. I've also tried to use common ingredients that can be found in most large grocery chains, Asian markets, or online.

As your new eating plan settles into your daily life, you'll come up with tricks of your own. I am confident that you'll be recreating your kids' grandma's recipes the new way in no time!

PART 1:
JJ BASE AND PREMADE PANTRY RECIPES

This section contains our JJ Base Blends, sauce, and other frequently used items that can easily be made at home, save money, and reduce preparation time.

# JJ Cake-Base Blend

This Base Blend is mostly used in fluffy and cakey texture baked goods, such as cakes, muffins, breads, pastry, etc.

Yield: 3 1/2 cups to 7 cups Prep time: 5 minutes

Ingredients

Ingredients	Small	Large
rice flour	2 cups	4 cups
tapioca starch	3/4 cup	1 1/2 cups
potato starch	3/4 cup	1 1/2 cups

Directions:

1. Add all ingredients to an airtight container. Whisk until ingredients are well combined.

2. Store in an airtight container in a dry, cool pantry.

Tips:

- The printout section contains a label recipe that you can print and tape right on your container.

 # JJ Cookie-Base Blend

This Base Blend is used to make dense texture baked goods, such as cookies, brownies, etc.

Yield: 3 3/4 cups to 7 1/2 cups Prep time: 5 minutes

 ## Ingredients

	Small	Large
sweet rice flour	1 1/2 cups	3 cups
rice flour	1 cup	2 cups
potato starch	3/4 cup	1 1/2 cups
tapioca starch	1/2 cup	1 cup

Directions:

1. Add all ingredients to an airtight container. Whisk until ingredients are well combined.

2. Store in an airtight container in a dry, cool pantry.

Tips:

- The printout section contains a label recipe that you can print and tape right on your container.

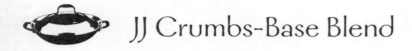

JJ Crumbs-Base Blend

This crumbs blend has a light coconut flavor. It tastes great in savory and sweet recipes.

Yield: 8 1/2 cups Prep time: 10 minutes

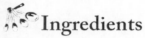

Ingredients

GF rice Chex cereal	1 14-ounce box
GF corn Chex cereal	1 14-ounce box
rice flour	4 cups
dried shredded coconut, unsweetened	1 cup

Directions:

1. Working in batches, place the rice and corn Chex cereals in the food processor bowl. Grind cereals to a powder or a fine texture similar to corn meal. Place ground cereal in a large air-tight container. Repeat with the remaining cereals.
2. Add the rice flour and dried coconut to the same container. Whisk the crumbs mixture until well combined.
3. Store in an airtight container and in the freezer to retain freshness.

 # JJ Sauce-Base

This basic sauce has a nice sweet, tangy, salty balance that can turn into many favorite sauces in no time! You'll save money by not having to buy many flavored sauce bottles.

Yield: 2 to 5 cups Prep time: 10 minutes

 ## Ingredients

Ingredients	Small	Large
ketchup	1 1/2 cups	3 cups
honey	2/3 cup	1 1/3 cups
rice vinegar	1/4 cup	1/2 cup
unsweetened pineapple juice	1/4 cup	1/2 cup
molasses	1/4 cup	1/2 cup
onion salt	1/2 tablespoon	1 tablespoon

Directions:

1. Stir all ingredients in a large saucepan, and bring it to boil over medium-high heat, stirring occasionally. Turn the heat to medium-low and continue to simmer for another 15 minutes, stirring occasionally.
2. Divide sauce in airtight containers and store in the refrigerator.

Tip:

- Apple cider vinegar can be substituted for rice vinegar. The taste will be slightly tangier.

Fried Shallots

Fried shallots make a great topping and add a mild savory flavor in many dishes. The boys and their friends love them on fried rice, soup, and noodle bowls.

This takes very little time if you can find "dried shallots" at the local Asian market. Don't buy the premade fried shallots, as many contain gluten and soy. I've included both dried shallots and fresh shallots methods, just in case.

Dried Shallots Method

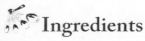## Ingredients

olive oil	1/4 cup
dried shallots	1 14-ounce package

Directions:

1. In a medium skillet, heat 1 tablespoon oil over medium heat.
2. Add about 1/2 cup of dried shallots, fry until golden brown, stirring frequently. Working in small batches will help get a nice even golden brown.
3. Remove shallots on to a baking sheet lined with paper towel. Continue with the next batch for the remaining dried shallots.
4. Store shallots in an airtight glass jar in the refrigerator. It will last a long time.

# Fresh Shallots Method

Ingredients

fresh shallots	14 to 16 large, thinly sliced
olive oil	1/4 cup

Directions:

1. Preheat oven 175 degrees F.
2. Spread shallots in a single layer on a large baking sheet.
3. Bake shallots in the oven on the top rack until shallots are dried, about 2 to 3 hours.
4. Follow the dried shallots method directions.

Five-Spice Powder

Five-Spice Powder is a specialized Asian spice, and you only need a small amount in the recipes. It's very easy to mix your own Five-Spice Powder, and it's less expensive. You can use store-bought Chinese Five Star Spice, although the recipe may taste slightly different depending on the manufacturers' ingredients.

Yield: 10 teaspoons Prep time: 5 minutes

 Ingredients

ground star anise	4 teaspoons
ground white pepper	2 teaspoons
ground cinnamon	2 teaspoons
ground ginger	1 teaspoon
ground cloves	1 teaspoon

 Directions:

1. Mix all ingredients until well blended, and store in an airtight spice jar.

Caramel Syrup

I use caramel syrup in many recipes in the book for flavoring and coloring.

Yield: 2/3 cup Prep time: 10 minutes

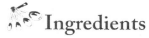

Ingredients

granulated sugar	1 cup
water	1/4 cup
water	5 tablespoons

Directions:

1. In a medium saucepan, stir together the granulated sugar and 1/4 cup water. Melt sugar mixture over high heat without stirring. Continue to boil until mixture turns to a dark brown color, about 5 to 6 minutes from boiling point.

2. Remove saucepan from heat. Carefully add the remaining 5 tablespoons of water, stir quickly with a silicon spatula until the water is dissolved into the caramel. Immediately pour syrup into a glass or ceramic jar. Allow to cool and close jar with an airtight lid. The cooled syrup consistency should be similar to molasses.

3. It will keep in your pantry for 3 to 4 months.

Tips:

- Premade caramel syrup is available for purchase in many Asian markets. Be sure that you can trust the manufacturer as not all ingredients may be listed.

Chicken Stock

Chicken stock is used in many recipes, yet it's so easy and a lot less expensive to make it yourself. This recipe is made without salt so that it can be seasoned according to the recipes.

 ## Ingredients

chicken breast with bones	3 pounds
carrots, cut into 2" length	4
celery, cut into 2" length	2 stems
onion	1 large

 ## Directions:

1. In large pan, add chicken and fill pan with water. Cook chicken over high heat until boiling, skimming the surface occasionally. Continue to cook until the stock is clear, about another 8 to 10 minutes. Remove pan from heat.

2. In a 4- or 5-quart slow cooker, transfer the chicken, stock, carrots, celery, and onion. Fill slow cooker with water and cook over low heat for 6 to 8 hours. Optionally, continue to cook chicken stock in pan over medium heat until chicken and vegetables are tender.

3. Allow stock to cool. Discard the chicken bones, carrots, celery, onion, and strain the stock through a sieve.

Tips:

- Freeze stock in 1-cup containers. Many sauces and recipes in the book call for 1 cup or less.
- A great way to save money is to reuse your small plastic containers to store stock.
- Another way to save is to use bones from a roast chicken or turkey dinner. Just skip the first step in the directions.
- All recipes in this book use this chicken stock recipe. If you prefer to purchase chicken stock, adjust the recipe's salt or fish sauce amount depending on the salt content in the purchased stock.

PART 2:
SAUCES

Sauces are a big part of many cultures' cuisines. The idea of eliminating soy leaves many folks feeling limited because it's in majority of premade sauces. This section contains sauces for dipping, seasoned sauces for condiments, and marinades.

Seasoned Fish Sauce

Seasoned fish sauce is used as a condiment sauce to season food similar to soy sauce—over rice, dipping sauce for eggrolls. I've made this basic sauce without the traditional lime juice and garlic for longer shelf life.

Yield: 4 cups Prep time: 10 minutes

 Ingredients

water	2 1/2 cups
fish sauce	3/4 cup
granulated sugar	1/2 cup
rice vinegar	1/3 cup

 Directions:

1. Boil the water. Set aside.
2. In a large container, add the fish sauce, granulated sugar, and rice vinegar. Stir in hot water until the sugar is dissolved. Store in the refrigerator until use.

This sauce can be served two ways:
- Basic. Spoon sauce over food or in a bowl for dipping.
- Dressed up. Stir 1/2 cup seasoned fish sauce, 1 minced garlic, 1 tablespoon finely shredded carrots, and 1/4 teaspoon chili peppers in a bowl. Spoon over food or use for dipping.

 Tips:

- The fish sauce ingredient refers to the concentrated fish sauce in a bottle that can be purchased from store. Read the label carefully as some newer products contain gluten, especially the premade seasoned sauce.

No-Soy Seasoned Sauce

Seasoned fish sauce is the primary dipping sauce at our house. This nutritious seasoned sauce is a great alternative for fermented soy sauce and also makes great pot sticker sauce.

Yield: 1 cup Prep time: 20 minutes

 Ingredients

dried oyster mushroom	1/2 ounce
boiling water	1 1/2 cups
garlic, smash and peel	10 cloves
brussels sprouts, cut in half	10 each
carrots, cut into 2" length	3 each
red bell pepper, seeded and cut into 2" pieces	1 small
red onion, quartered	1 small
dried thyme	1/2 tablespoon
olive oil	2 tablespoons
balsamic vinegar	1 tablespoon
caramel syrup	1/2 tablespoon
salt	2 1/4 teaspoons
vegetable or chicken stock, no salt (page 38)	1 1/2 cups

 **Directions:**

1. Preheat oven to 475 degrees F.
2. Place the dried oyster mushroom and 1 1/2 cups boiling water in a bowl to rehydrate. Set aside.
3. Toss together the garlic cloves, brussels sprouts, carrots, red bell peppers, red onion, dried thyme, olive oil, and balsamic vinegar in a large bowl until vegetables are coated.

4. Spread vegetables evenly single layer on a baking sheet. Bake 18 to 20 minutes, or until vegetables are tender and golden brown, stirring occasionally. Remove from oven.

5. Place roasted vegetables, caramel syrup, and salt in a large saucepan. Pour about 1/4 cup vegetable or chicken stock into the baking sheet, scrape up the brown bits, and pour the brown stock into the same saucepan. Add the remaining chicken stock, rehydrated mushrooms, and water into the same saucepan. Stir to combine ingredients.

6. Cook mixture to a boil over high heat. Change to medium heat setting and simmer for another 7 to 8 minutes. Remove from heat and let stand to cool, about 15 minutes.

7. Squeeze and filter the liquid through a sieve and discard the solids. Use sauce similar to soy sauce.

POT STICKER SAUCE

Heat 2/3 cup No-Soy Seasoned Sauce, 1 teaspoon sesame oil, 1 teaspoon rice vinegar, and 1/2 tablespoon granulated sugar over medium heat until sugar is dissolved. Remove from heat and top with sliced green onion over sauce. Serve warm.

Tips:

- Smash and peel garlic clove. Place a garlic clove on a cutting board; smash it by pressing the side of a large knife on it. The peel should come off easily.
- Pour 1 tablespoon of sauce in an ice cube tray, and freeze overnight. Remove frozen sauce cubes from tray, quickly transfer sauce cubes in a resealable plastic storage bag, and put them back in the freezer. Keep frozen until use. Take out only the amount you need.

Spring Roll Sauce

This recipe replaces the typical spring roll sauce made with hoisin sauce. It also tastes great over meatballs.

Yield: 1 1/3 cups Prep Time: 15 minutes

 Ingredients

JJ Sauce-Base	6 tablespoons
sweet potato pureed baby food, stage 1	4 tablespoons
prunes pureed baby food, stage 1	2 tablespoons
sesame oil	4 tablespoons
fish sauce	2 teaspoons
five-spice powder (page 36)	1 teaspoon
olive oil	2 tablespoons
garlic, minced	6 cloves
chicken stock, no salt (page 38)	1/2 cup
chopped peanuts (optional)	1 tablespoon

 Directions:

1. Stir together JJ Sauce-Base, sweet potato puree, prunes puree, sesame oil, fish sauce, and five-spice powder in a medium bowl until blended. Set aside.

2. In a medium saucepan, heat olive oil and garlic over medium-high heat until garlic is fragrant, about 20 seconds. Pour in the prepared sauce, chicken stock, and simmer on medium for another 2 minutes.

3. Serve warm with chopped peanuts.

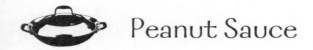

Peanut Sauce

Peanut sauce makes a delicious dipping sauce with chicken nuggets, spring rolls, and other finger foods.

Yield: 3/4 cups Prep time: 10 minutes

Ingredients

JJ Sauce-Base	3 tablespoons
chicken stock, no salt (page 38)	1/4 cup
creamy peanut butter	3 tablespoons
olive oil	1 teaspoon
garlic, minced	2 cloves
can coconut milk, light	1/4 cup

Directions:

1. Stir together the JJ Sauce-Base, chicken stock, and peanut butter in a medium bowl until combined. Set aside.
2. In a medium saucepan, heat olive oil and garlic over medium heat until garlic is fragrant, about 20 seconds. Pour in the peanut butter mixture and simmer on medium-low for another 2 minutes.
3. Remove saucepan from heat. Stir in the coconut milk until well combined.
4. Store in an airtight container in the refrigerator for up to 3 days. Or store in individual serving container in the freezer for up to 3 months. Serve warm or at room temperature.

Savory Tomato Sauce

Vietnamese tomato sauce has a lighter texture than the Italian pasta sauce. This tomato sauce is used over Xiu-Mai meatballs or over other dishes such as pan-fried fish.

Yield: 1 cup Prep Time: 10 minutes

 Ingredients

chicken stock, no salt (page 38)	1 cup
fish sauce	2 tablespoons
granulated sugar	1 tablespoon
tapioca starch	2 teaspoons
olive oil	2 tablespoons
tomato paste	3 tablespoons
onion, finely chopped	1/2 cup
garlic, minced	6 cloves
dried chili flakes	a pinch

 **Directions:**

1. Stir chicken stock, fish sauce, granulated sugar, tapioca starch in a bowl until tapioca starch is dissolved. Set aside.
2. In a medium skillet, heat olive oil over medium-high heat, stir in tomato paste, onion, garlic, and chili flakes. Continue to stir while frying for about 1 to 2 minutes.
3. Stir in the chicken stock mixture and simmer until sauce is thickened, about 2 to 3 minutes. Stir frequently.
4. Serve warm with Xiu-Mai meatballs or pan-fried fish.

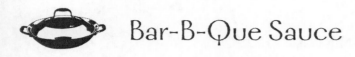

Bar-B-Que Sauce

My friend Karla gave me her family's favorite bar-b-que recipe. I modified it to use our JJ Sauce-Base.

Yield: 3/4 cup Prep time: 5 minutes

Ingredients

JJ Sauce-Base	1 cup
water	2 tablespoons
brown sugar	1 tablespoon
onion powder	1 teaspoon
yellow mustard	1 teaspoon
paprika	1/2 teaspoon
cayenne pepper	a pinch

Directions:

1. In a medium saucepan, heat all ingredients over medium-high heat until just bubbly.
2. Turn the heat to medium-low, simmer for another 5 minutes.
3. Remove from heat. Store in an airtight container in the refrigerator until use.

Tips:

- For a stronger kick, increase the amount of mustard or cayenne pepper.

Chipotle Sauce

Yield: 1/4 cup Prep time: 5 minutes

 Ingredients

JJ Sauce-Base	1/4 cup
dried minced onion	1 tablespoon
garlic powder	1/2 teaspoon
chipotle seasoning	1/2 to 1 teaspoon (1 tsp will give a little more kick)
cinnamon	1/4 teaspoon
mayonnaise	2 teaspoons (optional)

 Directions:

1. Stir all ingredients in a small bowl.
2. Let sauce stand 15 minutes in the refrigerator before use.
3. Use sauce over grilled meat, with sandwich or wrap, or as dipping sauce.

PART 3:
GRAB-N-GO

Life is busy! These foods can be prepared ahead and frozen. This way, you'll always be ready for last-minute parties or lunches. Some of these items can also be turned into quick-fix dinner for those late days at the office.

To save time! I usually make these in large-size batches as they only add a little more preparation and cleanup time than the small batch. These recipes are printed in both sizes for your convenience.

Chicken Nuggets

These delicious golden nuggets are not just for kid's lunch. They can quickly be turned into many American or Asian meals for the whole family. I actually double the large batch every time!

Yield: 6 to 18 servings Prep time: 30 to 40 minutes

Ingredients

Ingredients	Small	Large
chicken breast, skinless, boneless	3 pounds	9 pounds
eggs	1 large	3 large
rice milk	1/4 cup	3/4 cup
brown rice flour	1/3 cup	1 cup
dried parsley	1 teaspoon	1 tablespoon
salt	3/4 teaspoon	1 1/2 teaspoons
garlic powder	1/4 teaspoon	3/4 teaspoon
paprika	1/4 teaspoon	3/4 teaspoon
baking powder	1 teaspoon	1 tablespoon
JJ Crumbs-Base Blend	1 cup	3 cups
canola oil for frying		

Directions:

1. Cut chicken breast into nugget-size pieces and place in a large bowl.

2. In a separate bowl, whisk together the eggs, rice milk, brown rice flour, parsley, salt, garlic powder, and paprika until well combined. Whisk in baking powder until combined into mixture.

3. Pour seasoned mixture over the chicken. Fold mixture and chicken until all chicken pieces are soaked with seasoned mixture.

4. Work with small amount at a time, place some the JJ Crumbs-Base Blend on a large plate, coat chicken pieces with crumbs and transferred breaded chicken pieces to a baking sheet. Repeat with the remaining chicken pieces.

5. Preheat the oil in a heavy saucepan to 360 degrees F. Place breaded chicken into the hot oil, fry 7 to 8 minutes, or until golden.

Tips:

- When making large batch, set up two large pans for frying to reduce your frying time.
- Place nuggets in freezer storage bags and freeze until use.

Onion Corn Dogs

Green onions add a nice light savory flavor to the classic corndogs. The corndog-maker appliance makes a great alternative to the traditional deep-frying method.

Yield: 16 to 32 corn dogs Prep time: 20 to 25 minutes

Ingredients

Ingredients	Small	Large
JJ Cake-Base Blend	2 cups	4 cups
yellow cornmeal	1/4 cup	1/2 cup
baking powder	1 1/2 tablespoons	3 tablespoons
salt	3/4 teaspoon	1 1/2 teaspoons
xanthum gum	1/2 teaspoon	1 teaspoon
light olive oil	1/4 cup	1/2 cup
rice milk	1 cup	2 cups
maple syrup	3 tablespoons	6 tablespoons
eggs	2 large	4 large
green onion, finely sliced	1/2 cup	1 cup
hot dogs, cut into half	1 8-package	2 8-package

Directions:

1. Whisk together the JJ Cake-Base Blend, cornmeal, baking powder, salt, and xanthum gum in a large mixing bowl. Make a well in the center; add olive oil, rice milk, maple syrup, and eggs into the well. With an electric mixer, beat on low speed until mixture is just moist. Beat on high speed until batter is smooth, about 1 minute. The batter consistency is similar to a pancake batter. Fold in the green onion. Let batter rest for about 5 minutes.

2. If you're using a corndog-maker appliance, follow the appliance instructions.

3. For frying, heat oil in deep fryer to 365 degrees F. Pat dry with paper towels, and lay hot dogs on a baking sheet. Dust hot dogs with cornstarch. Dip hot dogs into batter and drop in the hot oil. Cook until batter is golden brown. Drain on paper towels.

Mini Meatballs Sub for Grab-N-Go: Make a batch of the Xiu-Mai meatballs (page 60). Replace the hotdogs with meatballs.

 Tips:
- Use extra batter to make breadsticks. Bake in the corndog-maker appliance.

Turkey Hot Pockets

This was the first successful recipe with pastry dough I ever made and is a family favorite since. The meat filling is a Vietnamese breakfast pastry, Banh Pate-So.

Yield: 50 pockets Prep time: 45 minutes

Ingredients

ground turkey	3 pounds
onion, finely chopped	3/4 cup
jicama, chopped	1 cup
granulated sugar	2 teaspoons
garlic powder	1 1/4 teaspoons
salt	1/2 teaspoon
olive oil	2 teaspoons
fish sauce	1 1/2 tablespoons
eggs	1 large
pastry crust (page 192)	1 batch

Directions:

1. Mix ground turkey, onion, jicama, granulated sugar, garlic powder, salt, olive oil, fish sauce, and eggs in a large bowl until well combined. Cover and place turkey mixture in the refrigerator while preparing the dough.

2. Preheat oven to 375 degrees F. Line baking sheet with parchment paper.

3. Prepare pastry dough. Follow the recipe for pastry dough.

4. Drizzle rice flour on work surface, roll out dough to about 1/4-inch thick. Place about 2 tablespoons turkey filling on dough, fold dough over filling, using a round biscuit cutter to cut into a half-moon shape, and seal the edges with a fork. Repeat with the remaining dough and turkey filling.

5. Place pocket on prepared baking sheet, and brush dough with olive oil. Bake pockets 25 to 28 minutes, or until golden brown.

6. Remove and cool pockets on wire rack.

Asian Bar-B-Que Pork Pocket. See recipe on page 56 for filling instructions. Follow above directions for making pockets.

Tips:

- The original recipe calls for ground pork. Reduce 1 tablespoon oil or more if ground pork or higher fat meat is used.
- Using a silicone pad and rolling pin will help reduce amount of flour needed for work surface.
- Three to four pockets can be made at a time by rolling the dough into a rectangular shape, placing fillings about 1/2 inch to 1 inch apart. Fold dough over fillings, and cut.
- Place cooled pockets in a freezer storage bag and store in freezer until use.

Asian Bar-B-Que Pork Puffs

Use your leftover Asian Bar-B-Que pork to make this quicker alternative to the bun-filled style.

Yield: 24 puffs Prep time: 30 minutes

Filling and Sauce Ingredients

chicken stock, no salt (page 38)	1 cup
JJ Sauce-Base	1/2 cup
brown sugar	6 tablespoons
rice flour	2 tablespoons
sesame oil	3 tablespoons
fish sauce	1 teaspoon
tomato paste	2 tablespoons
olive oil	2 teaspoons
garlic, minced	4 cloves
Asian Bar-B-Que Roast Pork, chop to small size	1/2 pound
green onion, finely sliced	1/2 cup

Puff Ingredients

JJ Cake-Base Blend	2 1/2 cups
brown rice flour	1/2 cup
baking powder	4 teaspoons
granulated sugar	4 teaspoons
xanthum gum	1 1/2 teaspoons
salt	1/2 teaspoon
eggs	6 large
rice milk	1 1/2 cups

Directions:

1. Stir the chicken stock, JJ Sauce-Base, brown sugar, rice flour, sesame oil, and fish sauce in a bowl until well combined and set aside.

2. In a medium skillet, stir-fry tomato paste in olive oil and garlic over medium-high heat until fragrant, for about 1 minute. Stir in the prepared sauce and cook until sauce is thickened. Pour half of the sauce into a container and reserve. Place the skillet back on the stove with the remaining half of the sauce, stir in green onion and diced pork until mixture is combined. Remove from heat and let stand to cool.

3. Preheat oven to 375 degrees F. Place paper baking cup in muffin pans or lightly grease muffin pans.

4. *For puff.* In a large mixing bowl, whisk together the JJ Cake-Base Blend, brown rice flour, baking powder, granulated sugar, xanthum gum, and salt. Beat in eggs and rice milk and with an electric mixer on low speed until just moist. Beat batter on medium until batter is smooth and thick, about 2 minutes.

5. Gently fold in the pork fillings to batter. Drop batter into the prepared muffin cups. Bake for 30 to 35 minutes, or until golden.

6. Remove from oven and cool on a wire rack. Serve warm with reserved sauce.

Tips:

- Wrap the cooled puffs tightly in a plastic wrap, put in a freezer bag, and store in the freezer.
- Divide remaining sauce in an ice cube tray, freeze for 3 to 4 hours, and quickly transfer frozen sauce cubes in a freezer storage bag with puffs.
- Plain roast pork or roast chicken can be substituted for the Asian Bar-B-Que Roast Pork.

Caramelized Pork Pizza

If you like big bold flavor, give our Asian pizza creation a try. This is made with the Vietnamese signature sweet and savory caramelized flavor.

Yield: 12 6-inch pizzas Prep time: 30 minutes

Ingredients

caramelized pork (page 97)	1 cup sauce, plus pork
tapioca starch	2 1/2 teaspoons
water	1/4 cup
pizza crust (page 194)	1 batch

Topping suggestions: shredded carrots, daikon, and chopped cilantro

Directions:

1. Preheat oven to 375 degrees F. Line two baking pans with parchment paper.
2. Separate the pork and caramelized sauce into separate bowls. Thinly slice the pork and set aside.
3. Stir together the tapioca starch and water in a small saucepan until starch is dissolved. Stir in the caramelized sauce and simmer over medium heat until sauce is slightly thickened. Remove from heat and set aside.
4. Prepare the pizza crust. Scoop about 1/4 cup batter onto the prepared baking pan using a #16 scoop. Spread batter to a flat round or square shape using a spreader spatula. Repeat with the remaining batter.
5. Top batter with sliced pork, prepared caramelized sauce, and desired toppings.
6. Bake 18 minutes, or until edges of crust are golden.
7. Remove from oven and cool on a wire rack.

For the classic pizza, top batter with pizza sauce, and desired toppings. Follow the above baking instructions.

🍵 Tips:

- Place pizza in a single layer on a baking sheet in the freezer for about 20 minutes. Remove from freezer, wrap each pizza tightly with plastic wrap, put in a freezer storage bag, and freeze until use.

Mini Xiu-Mai Meatball Sub

Xiu-Mai meatballs have a nice salty-sweet taste and no breadcrumbs!

Yield: 50 mini meatballs Prep time: 30 minutes

 ## Ingredients

ground pork	1 pound
ground chicken	1 pound
eggs	3 large
onion, finely chopped	1/2 cup
garlic, minced	3 cloves
granulated sugar	2 teaspoons
salt	3/4 teaspoon
caramel syrup	1/2 teaspoon
black pepper	1/4 teaspoon
Savory Tomato Sauce (page 45)	1 cup

 ## Directions:

1. Mix ground pork, ground chicken, eggs, onion, garlic, granulated sugar, salt, caramel syrup, and black pepper in a medium bowl until well combined. Cover the bowl with plastic wrap and refrigerator for 2 hours.
2. Preheat oven 400 degrees F.
3. Form meat mixture into meatballs by hand or use a 1-tablespoon scoop. Place meatballs on a baking sheet and bake for 15 minutes. Bigger meatballs will take a little longer, be sure to adjust baking times accordingly.
4. Prepare the Savory Tomato Sauce.
5. Simmer meatballs and savory tomato sauce in a large saucepan over medium-low heat and covered for 10 to 12 minutes.

Xiu-Mai Sub. Put meatballs in a mini baguettes, top with 2 spoons savory tomato sauce, add toppings (cucumbers, Jicama, sour daikon, carrots, cilantro), and serve.

Asian Meatballs for appetizer. Follow the above direction to make the meatballs. Replace the Savory Tomato Sauce with 2 cups of Spring Roll Sauce (page 43). Pour meatballs, Spring Roll Sauce in a slow cooker. Fold in 1 tablespoon sliced green onions and heat on low setting.

Tips:

- Make the remaining meatballs into sub-sandwiches (without sauce and toppings). Wrap each sub sandwich tightly in a plastic wrap; place in a freezer storage bag and store in freezer.

Turkey and Pork Cinnamon Patty (Cha Que)

This was the first recipe I've learned from my mom. It has many uses and convenience, which is great for on-the-go or a quick meal.

Yield: 15 to 30 servings Prep time: 20 to 25 minutes.

Ingredients

	Small	Large
ground turkey	1 pound	2 pounds
pork loin, trim excess fat, cut into 2" cubes	1 pound	2 pounds
potato starch	4 teaspoons	8 teaspoons
granulated sugar	1 teaspoon	2 teaspoons
salt	1/2 teaspoon	1 teaspoon
ground cinnamon	1/4 teaspoon	1/2 teaspoon
olive oil	3 tablespoons	6 tablespoons
ice-cold water	3 tablespoons	6 tablespoons
fish sauce	1 tablespoon	2 tablespoons
baking powder	1 tablespoon	2 tablespoons

Directions:

1. Mix ground turkey, pork loin, potato starch, granulated sugar, salt, cinnamon, olive oil, ice-cold water, and fish sauce in a large bowl. Stir in baking powder until well combined.

2. Working in small batches, place the meat mixture in the food processor bowl, process meat to a fine and smooth texture. Repeat with the remaining meat mixture.

3. Chill meat mixture in the freezer until firm, about 40 to 45 minutes.

4. Preheat oven to 350 degrees F. Lightly grease a 9x13 glass baking pan with olive oil. (Two baking pans for the large-size batch.)

5. Spread the meat mixture evenly into the baking pan with a spreader spatula. Bake 25 minutes. The center should bounce back if pressed down. Remove from oven and cool in pan on a wire rack.

6. Slice and serve. Serve warm or cold.

Tips:

- The original recipe uses pork fat. I replaced the pork fat with olive oil in this recipe to create a healthier result.
- Reduce or increase the amount of oil and water if your meat has a lot of fat or too lean. For best result, adjust 1 tablespoon each at a time. Test by grinding a small amount of the meat first. The texture should be firm and smooth, not tough or mushy.
- Cut into 6 or 8 square patties per baking pan. Wrap each patty tightly in plastic wrap, put in a freezer storage bag, and freeze until use. Thaw patty in the refrigerator.
- This can be eaten in many ways: in sandwiches, fried rice, salad, stir-fry, noodles, or even with crackers.

Egg Rolls (Cha Gio)

These classic traditional eggrolls are flavorful and disappear fast when we serve them to family or guests. They also make great appetizers and grab-n-go meals.

Yield: 55 to 60 eggrolls Prep time: 1 hour 30 minutes including rolling time.

Filling Ingredients

dried shredded black mushroom (optional)	2 tablespoons
cellophane noodles	2.5 ounces
ground chicken	1 pound
ground pork	1 pound
onion, finely chopped	2/3 cup
jicama, finely chopped	1 cup
carrots, shredded or finely chopped (optional)	1/2 cup
eggs	2 large
salt	1 teaspoon

Wrap Ingredients

6" or 12" rice paper wrappers cut in half	1 package
eggs	4 large
cornstarch	1 cup
water	1/2 cup
peanut or canola oil for frying	

Directions:

1. Soak the black mushroom in hot water in a small bowl until soft, about 5 minutes. Drain and chop.
2. In a separate bowl, soak the cellophane noodles with cold water until pliable, about 5 minutes. Drain and cut them into 2-inch lengths.
3. In a large bowl, mix the chicken, pork, black mushroom, cellophane noodles, onion, jicama, carrots, 2 eggs, and salt until well combined.
4. In a medium bowl, beat 4 eggs and 1/2 cup water until foamy.
5. Place cornstarch on a plate.
6. Lay a rice paper on a large dinner plate. Using a pastry brush, coat both sides with the egg wash mixture. Allow to stand a few seconds to soften. Put a heaping tablespoon of filling about 1/2" from the bottom straight edge of each rice paper. Fold the sides of wrapper over the filling tightly, tightly roll the wrapper and filling up toward the round edge to close eggroll. Roll eggrolls over the plate of cornstarch to coat. Place eggrolls on a baking sheet. Repeat with remaining fillings.
7. Heat 1" oil in a heavy large saucepan or deep fryer to 350 degrees. Fry about 8 to 10 rolls at a time until golden, about 9 to 10 minutes. Remove and drain on paper towels. Repeat with the remaining eggrolls.

Serve hot with Seasoned Fish Sauce (page 40), butter lettuce, cucumbers, and mint leaves.

Tips:

- To reduce wrapping time, use 2 dinner plates. Alternate the rolling of eggroll on one plate while waiting for the rice wrapper to soften on the other plate.
- The combination of ground pork and chicken is used to reduce fat. Recipe will work if you prefer to use all pork or all chicken.
- Place cooled eggrolls in a freezer storage bag and store in freezer until use.
- Reheat: Preheat oven to 300 degrees F. Place eggrolls in a single layer on an ungreased baking sheet. Heat for 8 to 10 minutes.
- Serving ideas: cut-up into bite-size and serve with rice or noodles with seasoned fish sauce.

# Spring Rolls (Goi Coun)

Spring rolls are a healthier alternative to the fried eggrolls. Each roll is like a mini-meal—noodles, meat, and fresh herbs.

Yield: 12 rolls Prep time: 30 to 40 minutes including wrapping time.

Ingredients

pork loin or shoulder (optional)	1/4 pound
dried rice vermicelli (bun noodles)	1/2 package
frozen precooked shrimps, tailed, deveined, and thawed	1/2 pound
lettuce, shredded	2 cups
fresh mint leaves	12 leaves
unsalted roasted peanuts, chopped	1/4 cup
6" rice paper wrappers	12
spring roll sauce (page 43)	

Directions:

1. Cook the pork in a small saucepan over medium-high heat until cooked through, about 12 to 15 minutes. Drain and let stand to cool in the refrigerator. Slice into thin slices.
2. Cook rice vermicelli following package direction. Rinse in cold water thoroughly, and set aside.
3. Rinse shrimps in cold water, place in a bowl, and set aside
4. In another bowl, combine shredded lettuce and chopped mint leaves. Set aside.
5. In a large bowl, fill with room-temperature water. Arrange your ingredients in an assembly line—shrimps, pork, vermicelli noodles, and lettuce-herbs.
6. Using 2 large dinner plates, dip a rice paper into the bowl of water, shake off excess water, and lay it on each plate. Allow to stand a few seconds to soften. Put 3 shrimps on the soft

rice wrapper about 1/2" from the bottom edge, top shrimps with a pork slice, a small amount of vermicelli, and lettuce-herbs. Fold the sides of wrapper over the fillings tightly, pressing down as you roll toward the edge to close the roll. Repeat with remaining wrappers and filling.

7. Serve immediately with Spring Roll Sauce.

Leftover meats also make delicious spring rolls:

Ginger Glazed Steak Rolls. Substitute the pork and shrimps for leftover Ginger Glazed Steak, follow above direction, and serve with Peanut Sauce (page 44).

Stir-Fry Rolls. Substitute the pork and shrimps for leftover stir-fry, follow above direction, and serve with Spring Roll Sauce.

Chipotle Chicken Rolls. Substitute the pork and shrimps for rotisserie or roast chicken, follow above direction, and serve with chipotle sauce.

Tips:

- The rice vermicelli noodles can be hard to work with once dry. This is a trick I've learned from my aunt Moon: Shortly after rinsing, use a fork and swirl the noodles into a small round shape just enough for each roll. Put each round on a plate until use.
- To keep the spring rolls moist until serving time, cover with a moist paper towel and tightly wrap with plastic wrap.
- These spring rolls get hard in the refrigerator; make just enough for your serving needs.

Pot Stickers

I've made this while helping out a friend. Her son loves pot stickers.

Yield: 20 to 25 pot stickers Prep time: 50 minutes including wrapping time.

Dough Ingredients

	Small	Large
JJ Cake-Base Blend	2 1/2 cups	5 cups
rice flour	1/2 cup	1 cup
xanthum gum	1 1/2 teaspoons	1 tablespoon
salt	1/2 teaspoon	1 teaspoon
hot water	2 to 3 cups	4 to 6 cups

Filling Ingredients

ground chicken	1 pound	2 pounds
napa cabbage, chopped	2 cups	4 cups
green onion, finely sliced	1/4 cup	1/2 cup
garlic powder	1 teaspoon	2 teaspoons
salt	1/2 teaspoon	1 teaspoon
caramel syrup	1 teaspoon	2 teaspoons
sesame oil	1 teaspoon	2 teaspoons
canola or peanut oil for frying		

Directions:

1. *For dough.* Boil water and set aside. Whisk the JJ Cake-Base Blend, rice flour, xanthum gum, and salt into a large mixing bowl. Make a well in the center of flour mixture, add the hot water, start with 2 cups first and then add 1 tablespoon at a time until dough is smooth but not sticking to bowl. Knead the dough for about 5 minutes. Cover dough with a moist paper towel and let it sit while making the filling.

2. *For filling.* Mix the chicken, napa cabbage, green onion, garlic powder, salt, caramel syrup, and sesame oil in a large bowl until well combined.

3. *Wrap pot stickers.* Work with a small ball of dough at a time on a lightly floured surface pad. Knead the dough 2 to 3 times; roll it out to about 1 mm thick. Using a dough cutter to cut the dough into a 5-inch circle.

4. Place a heaping tablespoon of the filling in the center of dough. Fold the dough in half, fold or press the edges together, and press the edges with a fork to seal. Brush a little water around the edge of the dough to help with seal as needed. Repeat wrapping pot stickers with remaining filling.

5. *Fry pot stickers.* Put about 2 tablespoon of canola oil in a medium-size skillet, put a single layer of pot stickers in the skillet. Fill the skillet with enough water to cover about half of the pot stickers. Cover skillet leaving a small opening for steam to escape, fry over medium heat for 10 minutes. After 10 minutes, remove lid, continue to fry pot stickers until the bottoms are golden brown. Remove from heat and repeat this step with the remaining pot stickers.

6. Serve with pot sticker sauce (page 42).

Tips:

- Place remaining chopped napa cabbage in a freezer storage bag and store in a freezer until use.
- Place single layer pot stickers on a baking sheet and in the freezer for 30 minutes. Transfer frozen pot stickers to a freezer storage bag and freeze until use.

PART 4:
DINNERS

The key with any home-cooked meal is to make it easier on you with preparation. Chances are that only 1 or 2 of your family members "need" to be on this diet. However, it is much easier to make one meal for the whole family instead of two. You'll save time and money in the end. Many of these main dishes have been served to family and dinner guests. Both have always enjoyed these foods.

I typically season food on the lighter side. This way, everyone can adjust the saltiness to their own preference at the table. Also, fish sauce can be strong for some folks; I've used a combination of fish sauce and salt to reduce the pungency and retain the traditional Vietnamese flavoring.

Planning for more than one meal ahead will save a lot of preparation time—chopping vegetables, slicing meat, and making extra to turn leftovers into another quick-fix meal or grab-n-go items. Look for these ideas in the "Tips" section of the recipes.

Chicken Pho Noodle Soup

Pho soup is a Vietnamese signature soup that has been a favorite among kids and adults. You'll need an 8- to 9-cm stainless steel filter-ball with this recipe.

Yield: 12 servings Prep time: 30 minutes

 Ingredients

chicken breast, bone-in	3 pounds
fresh ginger, sliced	1 1-inch
star anise	7 whole
cinnamon sticks	3 3-inch sticks
anise seeds	3 teaspoons
coriander	3 teaspoons
cardamom, whole	1 whole
onion	1 large
granulated sugar	2 teaspoons
dried pho rice noodles	1 14-ounce package
salt	1 1/2 tablespoons
fish sauce	2 tablespoons
green onion for garnish, sliced	

 Directions:

1. Place chicken and water in a large saucepan. Cook chicken over high heat until chicken is cook through, about 25 minutes. Skimming the surface occasionally.

2. Transfer cooked chicken to a cutting board to cool. Pour stock in a slow cooker.

3. Place the ginger, star anise, cinnamon sticks, anise seeds, coriander, and cardamom in the filter-ball, close tightly, and place filter-ball in the slow cooker.

4. Separate the chicken breast meat from the bones. Place the bones in the slow cooker.

5. Add whole onion, granulated sugar, and enough water to fill the slow cooker. Cook over low heat for 8 hours.
6. Slice chicken breast, place in a container, cover, and store in the refrigerator until use.
7. Follow package direction to cook pho noodles. Cook just enough noodles for needed servings.
8. Stir in salt and fish sauce in the last hour of cooking. Remove the bones, filter-ball, and onion. Filter the soup broth through a sieve. Discard all solids.
9. To serve. Place a handful of cooked pho noodles in a soup bowl, top with sliced chicken breast, and green onion. Spoon in pho broth over noodles. Serve hot.

Tips:

- The stainless steel filter-ball, whole cardamom and whole star anise can be found at most Asian market.
- 1 14-ounce dried pho noodles will make about 6 to 7 servings.
- Divide the remaining soup broth in a 3 to 4 serving containers and store in the freezer until use.

Chicken Rice Soup (Chao)

Chao is a comfort soup similar to chicken noodle soup. If you have premade chicken stock, you'll be able to whip this up in 5 minutes.

Yield: 4 servings Prep time: 20 minutes

Ingredients

chicken breast	2 to 3 fillets
water	6 cups
cooked rice	1 1/2 cups
salt	1/4 teaspoon
fried shallots	1 tablespoon
fish sauce	1 tablespoon
green onion for garnish, sliced	2 tablespoons

Directions:

1. In a large saucepan, cover chicken with 6 cups of water, and cook chicken over high heat until done, about 20 to 25 minutes. Skimming the surface occasionally. Transfer cooked chicken to a container, cover, and store in the refrigerator until use.
2. Stir in cooked rice, and salt to chicken stock. Bring soup to a boil over medium-high heat. Continue to cook over medium heat until liquid is thickened and rice is very soft, about 20 minutes. Stir in fried shallots, fish sauce, and continue to simmer for another 5 minutes.
3. Spoon rice soup in a bowl, top with sliced chicken breast and green onion and serve.

Tips:

- If you have premade chicken stock, skip the first step; use about 4 cups chicken stock and continue with step 2 of the direction.

 # Chicken Stew

This French-influence savory stew is usually made with rabbit and perfect for those cold days.

Yield: 4 servings Prep time: 20 minutes

 ## Ingredients

olive oil	2 tablespoons
onion, sliced	1/2 cup
garlic, minced	5 cloves
chicken thighs, remove skin	3 pounds
olive oil	1 teaspoon
tomato paste	3 tablespoons
chicken stock, no salt (page 38) or water	2 cups
white cooking wine	1/4 cup
salt	1 1/2 teaspoons
granulated sugar	1 teaspoon
baby carrots	2 cups
mushrooms, sliced	2 cups
bay leaves	2

Directions:

1. In a large heavy saucepan, stir and cook 2 tablespoons olive oil, onion, and garlic over medium-high heat until golden brown or caramelized, about 3 to 4 minutes. Transfer onions to a large plate.

2. Add chicken thighs to the saucepan and brown the chicken over medium-high heat, about 3 minutes on each side; add a little more oil if needed. Transfer chicken to the same plate with caramelized onion.

3. Add 1 teaspoon olive oil and tomato paste to saucepan, stir and cook about 30 seconds. Stir in chicken stock, cooking wine, salt, and granulated sugar. Scrape the brown bits and cook for about 1 minute. Add the chicken, caramelized onion, baby carrots, mushrooms, and bay leaves to saucepan and bring liquid to a boil. Cover saucepan, reduce heat to medium-low, and simmer until chicken is tender, about 45 minutes.

4. Serve with bread, over rice or pasta.

Basic Chicken Stir-Fry

This stir-fry recipe is a great crowd pleaser and is an excellent way to get your kids to enjoy veggies!

Yield: 4 servings Prep time: 20 minutes

 Ingredients

onion, quartered	1 medium
green or red bell peppers, seeded and chopped	1 medium
garlic, minced	3 cloves
salt	1/2 teaspoon
fish sauce	1/2 tablespoon
caramel syrup	1/2 teaspoon
sesame oil	1 teaspoon
chicken stock, no salt (page 38)	1 cup
sweet rice flour	1 tablespoon
olive oil, divided	3 tablespoons
chicken breast, thinly sliced	2 pounds
green onion, cut into 1" length	3 stems

 **Directions:**

1. Place onion, bell pepper, and minced garlic in a bowl. Set aside.
2. In a separate bowl, stir together salt, fish sauce, caramel syrup, and sesame oil. Set aside.
3. In separate bowl, stir together chicken stock and sweet rice flour until flour is dissolved. Set aside.
4. *Stir-Fry.* In a wok, heat 1 tablespoon olive oil around the sides of the wok over high heat. Stir-fry half of the chicken until lightly brown, about 4 minutes. Transfer cooked chicken to a plate. Add another 1 tablespoon olive oil to wok, repeat stir-frying the remaining chicken and transfer to the same plate.

5. Add the remaining 1 tablespoon olive oil to the wok, stir-fry onion, bell peppers, and garlic for 2 to 3 minutes. Stir in green onions and continue to stir-fry until vegetables are tender and crisp, about 2 minutes. Transfer cooked vegetables to the same plate with the chicken.

6. Pour the chicken stock mixture into the wok, stir continuously until sauce is thickened. Add chicken and vegetables to wok, stir-fry for 1 minute to heat through. Transfer to serving plate and serve immediately.

Garlic ginger stir-fry. Replace fish sauce, salt, caramel syrup, and chicken stock with 1 cup of No-Soy Seasoned Sauce, 1/2 teaspoon ground ginger, and increase garlic to 5 cloves.

Tips:

- You can simply change this basic recipe for your favorite meat and veggies.
- Use leftover to make into stir-fry noodle bowls, stir-fry salad, or spring rolls.

Honey Sesame Chicken

Turn your premade frozen chicken nuggets into this quick and tasty dinner in no time.

Yield: 4 servings Prep time: 15 minutes

Ingredients

frozen chicken nuggets	30 to 32 nuggets
water	1/2 cup
rice flour	1 1/2 tablespoons
chicken stock, no salt (page 38)	1 cup
JJ Sauce-Base	1/4 cup
dried minced onion	1 tablespoon
sesame oil	3 1/2 tablespoons
honey	3 tablespoons
garlic, minced	2 cloves
salt	1/2 teaspoon
sesame seeds	1 teaspoon

Directions:

1. Preheat oven to 350 degrees F.
2. Skip this step if your chicken nuggets are not frozen. Place frozen chicken nuggets in a 9x13 glass baking pan, cover with foil, and put in oven to warm, about 10 minutes.
3. Stir together water and rice flour in a bowl until flour is dissolved. Set aside.
4. In a medium saucepan, stir together the chicken stock, JJ Sauce-Base, dried onion, sesame oil, honey, garlic, and salt. Cook mixture over medium-high heat until bubbly, stir in the rice flour-water mixture. Cook and stir until sauce is bubbly and slightly thickened, about another minute.

5. Remove chicken from oven, uncover, pour sesame sauce over chicken, toss to coat chicken with sauce, and sprinkle sesame seeds over chicken. Cover pan with foil and return chicken to oven. Bake 5 to 8 minutes, or until nuggets are heated. Remove from oven.

Tips:

- If chicken nuggets are not available in your freezer, cut up about 1 to 1 1/2 pounds of chicken breast into bite-size pieces, coat chicken pieces with potato starch, stir-fry chicken until golden brown. Continue with step 3 of the direction.

 # Simple Chicken Sauté

This recipe is based on the meat filling of a Vietnamese signature crepe (Banh Cuon). It's very similar to the Thai lettuce wrap.

Yield: 4 servings Prep time: 20 minutes

 ## Ingredients

dried black mushroom	1 tablespoon
onion, finely chopped	1/4 cup
garlic, minced	3 cloves
water	1/4 cup
sweet rice flour	2 tablespoons
fish sauce	1 1/2 tablespoons
caramel syrup	1 teaspoon
salt	1/4 teaspoon
olive oil	1 tablespoon
ground chicken	1 pound
water chestnut, drain and chop	1 8-ounce can
green onion, sliced	1 stem

 ## Directions:

1. Rehydrate the dried black mushrooms in a bowl cover with warm water. Let stand for 5 minutes, or until softened. Drain and chop mushroom. Place chopped black mushroom, onion, and garlic in a bowl. Set aside.
2. In a separate bowl, stir together the water and sweet rice flour until combined. Set aside.
3. In a separate bowl, stir fish sauce, caramel syrup, and salt together. Set aside.
4. In a wok or large skillet, stir-fry black mushroom, onion, garlic, and olive oil over high heat until fragrant.

5. Stir in ground chicken, cook and break up chicken with a spatula until the chicken is no longer pink, about 4 to 5 minutes.
6. Stir in water chestnut and cook for another minute. Stir in green onion and fish sauce-caramel mixture until combined. Pour rice flour-water mixture over chicken. Stir and cook until chicken mixture is slightly thickened. Remove from heat.
7. Serve over cooked rice, or wrap in lettuce with Seasoned Fish Sauce.

Grilled Chicken Noodle Bowl

This is a simple noodle bowl meal made with chicken and fresh veggies and herbs. I was pleasantly surprised by how much the boys and their friends like this authentic dish.

Yield: 4 to 5 servings Prep time: 25 minutes

Ingredients

skinless, boneless chicken thighs	1 pound
onion, thinly sliced	1/4 cup
garlic, minced	3 cloves
granulated sugar	2 teaspoons
fish sauce	2 tablespoons
olive oil	1 tablespoon
lime juice	1/2 tablespoon
sesame oil	1 teaspoon
Five-Spice Powder	1/4 teaspoon
dried rice vermicelli (bun noodles)	1 package
honey	2 tablespoons
warm water	1 teaspoon

Accompaniments

shredded lettuce, cucumber slices, mint leaves	
fried shallots	1/4 cup
roasted peanuts, for toppings (optional)	1/4 cup
seasoned fish sauce (page 40)	

Directions:

1. Clean chicken, trim fat, and pat dry with a paper towel. Place chicken in a plastic resealable plastic storage bag.
2. Mix together the onion, garlic, granulated sugar, fish sauce, olive oil, lime juice, sesame oil, and Five-Spice Powder in a bowl; mix well. Pour marinade over chicken and seal bag. Marinade in refrigerator overnight or for at least 4 hours.
3. Cook the rice vermicelli according to package direction. Drain and rinse in cold water thoroughly and set aside.
4. Remove marinated chicken about 15 minutes before cooking. Stir together the honey and warm water in a bowl. Set aside.
5. Grill or broil on high about 8" to 10" from heat. Grill/broil about 5 to 6 minutes on each side, turning once.
6. Brush chicken with honey mixture, broil another 1 minute. Repeat on the other side. Remove from heat. Wait for 5 minutes and thinly slice chicken.
7. *To serve.* In a serving bowl, add a handful of vermicelli, top with sliced chicken, fried shallots, and crushed peanuts if used. Pour 3 to 4 heaping spoons of seasoned fish sauce over noodle bowls.

Tips:

- Use extra chicken to make Combination-Rice plate for another meal. Serve grilled chicken over rice with sliced cucumbers, tomatoes, fried onion, and seasoned fish sauce.
- For quicker meal, the grilled chicken in this recipe can be substituted with many leftover meats from another meal, including stir-fry.

Honey Orange Glazed Chicken

This chicken works well for a family dinner or for a big crowd. They go fast!

Yield: 4 to 5 servings Prep time: 30 minutes

Ingredients

JJ Sauce-Base	2/3 cup
orange juice	1/2 cup
honey	3 tablespoons
sesame oil	1 tablespoon
caramel syrup	1 teaspoon
garlic, minced	4 cloves
onion salt	1 1/2 teaspoons
ground ginger	1/4 teaspoon
boneless, skinless chicken thighs and breasts, cut into bite size	3 pounds

Directions:

1. Stir together the JJ Sauce-Base, orange juice, honey, sesame oil, caramel syrup, garlic, onion salt, and ginger; mix well. Reserve 1/2 cup of marinade in a container and store in the refrigerator.

2. Place chicken pieces in a resealable plastic storage bag, pour remaining marinades over chicken, and marinade in the refrigerator overnight, turning occasionally.

3. Remove chicken from refrigerator about 15 minutes before cooking. Preheat oven to 400 degrees F. Move oven rack to the center rack. Lightly grease two baking sheets with olive oil.

4. Arrange chicken pieces in a single layer on prepared baking sheets and discard the liquid. Bake chicken for 10 minutes; stir chicken with a spatula once.

5. Remove chicken from oven, change oven to broil on high. Discard juice and dripping from baking pan. Brush the 1/2 cup reserved honey-orange marinade over chicken pieces. Put chicken in the oven and broil until sauce is glazed, about 2 to 3 minutes.

6. Remove from oven and serve immediately.

Tips:

- Use extra chicken to make savory puffs.

No-Soy Teriyaki Chicken Kabobs

(picture on cover page)

Teriyaki without soy sauce? No problem! Another favorite with family and guests.

Yield: 6 servings Prep time: 20 minutes

Ingredients

chicken stock, no salt (page 38)	2/3 cup
JJ Sauce-Base	1/2 cup
maple syrup	1/4 cup
caramel syrup (optional)	1 tablespoon
onion salt	2 teaspoons
sesame oil	1 teaspoon
garlic, minced	4 cloves
ground ginger	1/4 teaspoon
boneless, skinless chicken breast, cut into 2" cubes	3 pounds
red onion, cut into 2" pieces	1 large
red bell peppers, cut into 2" pieces	1
green bell peppers, cut into 2" pieces	1
olive oil	2 tablespoons
apricot preserve	1 tablespoon
tapioca starch	1/2 teaspoon

Directions:

1. In a saucepan, whisk together chicken stock, JJ Sauce-Base, maple syrup, caramel syrup, onion salt, sesame oil, garlic, and ginger. Heat marinade over medium heat until bubbly; continue to simmer until sauce is slightly thickened, about 2 minutes. Remove from heat and let stand to cool.

2. Place chicken, onion, red and green bell peppers in a large plastic resealable plastic storage bag. Pour in olive oil and 3/4 cup of the cooled marinade over chicken and vegetables. Marinade overnight or for at least 4 hours in the refrigerator. Reserve and store the remaining marinade in the refrigerator.

3. Remove chicken from refrigerator and let stand at room temperature for 15 minutes. Thread chicken and vegetables alternately onto skewers, about 6 skewers. Discard juice.

4. Follow your grill instructions and grill kabobs until chicken is done.

5. In a saucepan, whisk the reserved marinade, apricot preserve, and tapioca starch over medium heat 2 to 3 minutes, or until sauce is slightly thickened. Serve sauce over chicken kabobs.

Tips:

- Substitute the chicken and veggies for your favorites.
- Cut up extra vegetables to make stir-fry for another dinner.
- Sauce may be used with other recipe calls for teriyaki. Depending on the recipe, the amount of chicken stock may need to be adjusted.

 # Roast Chicken (Ga Quay)

This Vietnamese version of roast chicken recipe can be prepared with a whole chicken or chicken parts.

Yield: 4 servings Prep time: 20 minutes

Ingredients

chicken thighs and drumsticks	2 1/2 to 3 pounds
garlic, minced	3 cloves
dark brown sugar	2 tablespoons
onion powder	1/2 teaspoon
salt	1/2 teaspoon
Five-Spice Powder (page 36)	1/4 teaspoon
fish sauce	2 tablespoons
olive oil	1 tablespoon
caramel syrup	1 teaspoon
water	1/2 to 1 cup
honey	3 tablespoons
water	2 tablespoons

Directions:

1. Place cleansed chicken in a large plastic resealable plastic storage bag.
2. Stir together the garlic, brown sugar, onion powder, salt, Five-Spice Powder, fish sauce, olive oil, and caramel syrup in a separate bowl; mix well. Pour marinade over chicken, and toss to coat chicken with marinade. Marinade overnight or at least 4 hours in the refrigerator; turn occasionally.
3. Preheat the oven to 375 degrees F. Move oven rack to the center.

4. Pour about 1/2 to 1 cup of water into the bottom of a roasting pan. Place chicken pieces on the top roasting pan. Roast chicken pieces until internal temperature reached 165 degrees, about 35 to 40 minutes, turn chicken at least once.

5. Stir together honey and water in a bowl; mix well. Remove chicken from oven, change oven to broil on high. Brush honey glazed over chicken, return chicken to oven, and broil for 2 minutes on each side of chicken.

Tips:

- Use extra roast chicken to make noodle bowl (page 83), fried rice (page 112), or sandwiches.

Baked Orange Chicken

This is another quick way to enjoy citrus chicken when you don't have the JJ Sauce-Base prepared.

Yield: 5 to 6 servings Prep time: 15 minutes

Ingredients

chicken thighs, bone-in	3 pounds
onion, thinly sliced	1/4 cup
orange juice	3/4 cup
garlic, minced	6 cloves
honey	3 tablespoons
fish sauce	2 tablespoons
olive oil	1 tablespoon
sesame oil	2 teaspoons
caramel syrup	1 teaspoon
ground ginger	1/2 teaspoon
orange, sliced (optional)	1

Directions:

1. Place cleansed chicken and onion in a resealable plastic storage bag.
2. Stir together orange juice, garlic, honey, fish sauce, olive oil, sesame oil, caramel syrup, and ginger in a small bowl; mix well. Pour marinade over chicken, and refrigerate overnight, turning occasionally.
3. Take chicken out of the refrigerator 15 to 20 minutes before baking.
4. Preheat oven to 400 degrees F. Place the orange slices on the bottom of a 9x13 baking pan, place chicken pieces on top of the orange slices skin side up, place onions from the marinade around chicken pieces, and discard the marinade liquid. Cover and bake chicken for about 20 minutes. Uncover pan and continue to bake 20 to 25 minutes, or chicken register at 165 degrees F or no longer pink.
5. Serve hot over rice.

Sweet Rice Stuffed Chicken

My mom used to make this into a stuffed deboned chicken for Thanksgiving. This is another way to enjoy this dish without having to deboned the chicken.

Yield: 8 servings   Prep time: 45 minutes

Ingredients

Stuffing and Chicken

cooked sweet rice	2 cups
cellophane noodles	1 2.5-ounce package
ground pork	1/2 pound
olive oil	1 teaspoon
mushrooms, chopped	1 cup
onion, finely chopped	1/2 cup
boneless chicken breast, halves length wise	4
margarine, melted and divided	2 tablespoons
JJ Crumbs-Base Blend	1/4 cup

Gravy

chicken stock, no salt	1 1/2 cup
rice flour	2 tablespoons
margarine	1 tablespoon
caramel syrup	1/2 teaspoon
salt	1/4 teaspoon

Directions:

1. Cook sweet rice following package instruction. Let stand to cool.
2. Preheat oven to 375 degrees F. Drizzle 1 tablespoon of melted margarine over the bottom of a 9x13 glass baking pan.
3. In a medium bowl, cover the cellophane noodles with cold water until pliable, about 5 minutes. Drain and cut into 1-inch length. Set aside.
4. In a medium-size skillet, heat olive oil over medium-high heat. Stir in ground pork crumbling it with the back of a wooden spoon, stirring frequently until pork is browned, about 8 to 10 minutes. Drain the fat. Stir in mushrooms, onion, and cook for 2 to 3 more minutes. Remove from heat.
5. In a large bowl, mix the cooked sweet rice, cellophane noodles, and pork mixture; mix stuffing well.
6. Place each chicken breast half on a thick cutting board, cover with a clear plastic wrap. Working from the center to edges, pound lightly with the flat side of the mallet to form 1/8-inch thick. Remove the plastic wrap; place a mound of the sweet rice stuffing on chicken, roll chicken over the stuffing jellyroll style, and place the exposed end of the chicken down on the prepared baking pan. Repeat with the remaining chicken breasts.
7. Drizzle remaining melted margarine over chicken, and sprinkle JJ Crumbs-Base Blend over chicken. Cover with foil and bake for 10 minutes, remove the foil and continue to bake another 8 to 10 minutes, or until chicken is no longer pink. Switch the oven heat to broil, and broil chicken on high for 2 minutes. Remove from oven. Let chicken stand for 5 minutes before slicing.
8. *For Gravy.* Whisk chicken stock, rice flour, margarine, caramel syrup, and salt in a saucepan. Cook and whisk gravy over medium heat until bubbly and thickened.

Tips:

- Most sweet rice package instruction is to steam the sweet rice. For this recipe, you can use a rice cooker if you have one.
- The gravy can be made for other classic American roast pork or chicken dishes. This stuffing can be used with pork or turkey.
- Most ground pork comes in a 1-pound package, brown the whole pound and freeze the remaining half for next time or another meal.

Herb Grilled Chicken

I am always looking for quick recipes. My sister-in-law got this recipe from the *Junior League Centennial Cookbook, 1996*. It was submitted by Udderly Delicious, Racine, Wisconsin, and required very little modification for the diet.

Yield: 4 Prep time: 10 minutes

 Ingredients

chicken thighs and drumsticks	2 to 2 1/2 pounds
dried basil	2 teaspoons
dried thyme	2 teaspoons
salt	1 1/2 teaspoons
paprika	2 teaspoons
garlic powder	1 teaspoon
olive oil	3/4 cup
lemon juice	3/4 cup

 Directions:

1. Place cleansed chicken in a resealable plastic storage bag.
2. Stir the basil, thyme, salt, paprika, garlic powder, olive oil, and lemon juice; mix well.
3. Pour marinade mixture over chicken, and seal bag. Marinate chicken in the refrigerator overnight or at least 4 hours.
4. Follow your grill instructions and grill chicken until done. Baste chicken often with the marinade.

Creamy Onion Mushroom Chicken

The fried shallots really give this classic American casserole dish a flavorful dinner.

Yield: 6 servings Prep time: 40 minutes

Ingredients

Mushroom soup

rice flour	1/4 cup
rice milk	1/2 cup
chicken stock, no salt (page38)	3/4 cup
mushroom	1 4-ounce can
salt	1/4 teaspoon

Remaining ingredients

JJ Crumbs-Base Blend	1/4 cup
salt	1 1/2 teaspoons
chicken breast, halves	3 pounds
olive oil	3 to 4 tablespoons
plain coconut yogurt	1/2 cup
hummus, plain	1/2 cup
lemon juice	2 teaspoons
fried shallots	2 tablespoons

Directions:

1. Preheat oven to 375 degrees F.
2. *For mushroom soup.* In a medium saucepan, stir the rice flour and rice milk together until flour is dissolved. Stir in chicken stock, mushroom water from can, and 1/4 teaspoon salt

into the saucepan. Whisk mixture continuously over medium-high heat until soup is slightly thickened, about 3 to 4 minutes. Stir in mushroom pieces and cook for another 2 minutes. Remove from heat and let stand to cool.

3. Mix the JJ Crumbs-Base Blend, and 1 1/2 teaspoons salt together in a plastic bag. Working in small batches, place chicken into bag, seal, and shake to coat chicken.

4. In a large skillet, brown both sides of chicken in olive oil over medium-high heat, 1 to 2 minutes each side, or until golden brown. Place browned chicken in a 9x13 glass or ceramic baking pan.

5. Whisk coconut yogurt, hummus, lemon juice, and fried shallots into the mushroom soup. Mix well. Pour soup mixture over chicken.

6. Cover baking pan with foil and bake for 45 minutes to 1 hour depending on thickness chicken pieces.

# Caramelized Pork (Thit Kho)

This rich brown sauce has a slightly sweet and savory flavor is popular with both kids and adults. It was a stable food at my mom's house and now at our house.

Yield: 6 to 8 servings Prep time: 25 minutes

Ingredients

pork shoulders, trim excess fat and cut into 2" cubes	3 pounds
olive oil, divided	1 tablespoon
onion, chopped	1/3 cup
garlic, minced	3 cloves
black peppers	a pinch
caramel syrup	3 tablespoons
fish sauce	3 1/2 tablespoons
unsweetened coconut juice	1 11.5-ounce container

## Directions:

1. In a large heavy saucepan, brown pork with 1/2 tablespoon olive oil over high heat until pork is no longer pink. Drain, discard the brown liquid, and rinse pork.

2. Place the cleansed pork and saucepan back on the stove. Stir in the remaining olive oil, onion, garlic, black peppers. Brown pork over high heat, about 4 minutes. Reduce heat to medium-high, stir in the caramel syrup until caramel covers pork pieces, add in fish sauce, coconut juice, and enough water just to the same level as the pork.

3. Bring mixture to a boil, cover with a little opening for steam to escape, and simmer over medium heat for about 20 minutes. Uncover and continue to simmer until meat is tender, stirring occasionally, another 15 minutes.

4. To serve. Pour a few spoons of meat and sauce over rice. Fresh cucumbers go great on the side.

Tips:

- Water may be substituted for coconut juice. The taste may change slightly.
- Divide the remaining pork and juice in a 1-cup or 2-cup containers. Store in freezer for another meal.
- Use extra pork to make Caramelized Pork Pizza (page 58).

 # Pork Chops and Tomato Sauce

These pork chops can be served plain or with tomato sauce.

Yield: 4 servings Prep time: 15 minutes

 ## Ingredients

garlic, minced	4 cloves
onion, thinly sliced	1/4 cup
brown sugar	2 tablespoons
olive oil, divided	2 tablespoons
fish sauce	1/2 tablespoon
sesame oil	1 teaspoon
caramel syrup	1/2 teaspoon
salt	1/4 teaspoon
boneless pork chops, 1/2" thick	1 1/2 pounds

 ## Tomato Sauce

chicken stock, no salt (page 38)	1/2 cup
petite cut diced tomato no salt, drained*	1 14.5-ounce can
salt	1/2 teaspoon
garlic powder	1/4 teaspoon
granulated sugar	1/4 teaspoon

 ## Directions:

1. Stir together the garlic, onion, brown sugar, 1 tablespoon olive oil, fish sauce, sesame oil, caramel syrup, and salt in a bowl; mix well. Set aside.

2. Poke the pork chops with a fork a few times and on both sides. Rub pork chops with the marinade. Place pork chops and remaining marinade in a resealable plastic storage bag. Marinade in the refrigerator overnight, turning occasionally.

3. Take pork chops out of the refrigerator about 15 minutes before cooking time. Move the oven rack to the middle rack and turn the broiler to high. Reserve the sliced onion from the marinade and discard the marinade liquid.

4. In a large skillet, heat 1 tablespoon of olive oil over medium-high heat. Brown the pork chops until golden, about 2 minutes on each side. Transfer the pork chops to an ovenproof baking pan. Broil pork chops in the oven until the meat thermometer registers 160 degrees F, about 5 to 6 minutes. Turn the pork chops once about half way. Remove from oven and keep warm.

5. Prepare tomato sauce while the pork chops are in the oven. In the same skillet, drain the fat, stir-fry the reserved onion over medium-high heat until brown. Stir in the chicken stock and scrape the brown bits, about 1 minute. Stir in the tomatoes, salt, garlic powder, and granulated sugar. Stir and cook tomato mixture to a boil. Turn the heat to medium and simmer sauce until thickened, about 1 minute.

6. Serve tomato sauce over the pork chops.

Tips:

- 1 large fresh tomato can be substituted for the can diced tomato. Slice tomato, remove the seeds, and chopped.
- This tomato sauce is also great over pan-fry fish or chicken.

Asian Bar-B-Que Roast Pork

Making Asian Bar-B-Que pork is a lot easier than it seems.

Yield: 5 to 6 servings Prep time: 15 minutes

Ingredients

JJ Sauce-Base	1/2 cup
brown sugar	2 tablespoons
onion salt	1/2 teaspoon
Five-Spice Powder (page 36)	1/2 teaspoon
pork tenderloin, cut into 2" to 3" wide.	2 pounds
garlic, minced	4 cloves
black peppers	a pinch
maple syrup	1 tablespoon

Directions:

1. Stir together the JJ Sauce-Base, brown sugar, onion salt, and Five-Spice Powder until well combined.

2. Poke holes all over pork using a fork, rub pork with garlic and black peppers. Place pork in a large resealable plastic storage bag, pour marinade over pork, and refrigerate overnight, turning occasionally.

3. Remove pork from the refrigerator about 15 minutes before roasting. Preheat oven to 425 degrees F.

4. Fill the bottom of roasting pan with water. Place the pork on the top roasting pan, and reserve the marinade for basting. Roast pork until a meat thermometer inserted into the thickest part register 160 degrees F, about 20 to 25 minutes. While roasting, brush pork 2 to 3 times with reserved marinade and turning once. Turn the oven to broil, and broil on high for about 2 minutes to glaze the sauce. Remove from oven, lightly brush maple syrup over pork, and let stand for 10 minutes before slicing.

Tips:

- Extra roast pork can be used to make Pork and Shrimp Pho-Noodles (page 103), fried rice (page 112), Asian Bar-B-Que Pork Puff (page 56) or pocket, or sandwiches.

Pork and Shrimp Sauté Noodle (Pho Xao)

Yield: 6 to 8 servings Prep time: 30 minutes

Ingredients

dried pho noodle	1 16-ounce package
chicken stock, no salt (page 38)	2 cups
fish sauce	3 tablespoons
sesame oil	1 tablespoon
caramel syrup	2 teaspoons
salt	1/2 teaspoon
onion, sliced	1/2 cup
garlic, minced	3 cloves
olive oil, divided	3 tablespoons
bok choy, coarsely chopped	3 cups
tomato, cut into 8 wedges	1 medium
red bell peppers, seeded and chopped (optional)	1
rice flour	1 tablespoon
eggs, lightly beaten	2 large
boneless pork chopped, thinly sliced	1 pound
frozen cooked shrimp, tailed, peeled, deveined, and thawed	1/2 pound

Directions:

1. Soaked noodles in hot water until pliable. Rinse to remove some of the starch. Lightly oil your hands and toss the noodles a few times. Set aside.

2. Stir together chicken stock, fish sauce, sesame oil, caramel syrup, and salt. Set aside.

3. In a wok, heat 1/2 tablespoons oil over medium-high heat. Stir-fry onion and garlic until onion until golden brown, about 2 minutes.

4. Stir in bok choy and cook until vegetables are just wilted, about 2 minutes.

5. Add tomato wedges and stir-fry for another 1 minute. Push vegetables around the sides of the wok, add 1/2 tablespoon of olive oil in the center of the wok, scramble eggs, and toss together with vegetables. Transfer to a plate.

6. Add 1 tablespoon olive oil to wok. Stir-fry the pork until juices run clear, about 3 to 5 minutes. Add shrimp and stir-fry for another minute. Transfer to the plate with the vegetables.

7. Add the remaining 1 tablespoon olive oil and chicken stock mixture to wok. Stir until continuously until sauce is thickened, about 2 minutes.

8. Stir-fry noodles and stir-fry until transparent and tender yet firm, about 4 to 5 minutes. Return the meat and vegetables to wok, and toss to combine ingredients. Remove from heat and serve.

Tips:

- Replace the pork chops with leftover Asian Bar-B-Que Pork Roast for quicker preparation. Slice roast pork into strips. Skip step 4. Add pork and shrimps with vegetables in step 5.
- Freeze unused chopped bok choy in freezer bag for next time or other recipes.

Ginger Glazed Steak

This is a very simple rub, and the glaze adds a subtle citrus flavor.

Yield: 4 to 5 servings Prep time: 20 minutes

 Ingredients

garlic, minced	3 cloves
olive oil	1 tablespoon
brown sugar	1 teaspoon
salt	1/2 teaspoon
black pepper	1/4 teaspoon
onion, thinly sliced	1/4 cup
sirloin steak	2 pounds

 Ginger Glaze

JJ Sauce-Base	1/2 cup
orange juice	1 tablespoon
sesame oil	2 teaspoons
garlic, minced	4 cloves
ground ginger	1 teaspoon
ground anise (optional)	1/8 teaspoon

 Directions:

1. Mix garlic, olive oil, brown sugar, salt, and black peppers. Stir in sliced onion. Rub mixture on both sides of the meat. Wrap meat tightly with plastic wrap and store in the refrigerator for at least 2 hours.

2. *For Ginger Glaze.* Stir JJ Sauce-Base, orange juice, sesame oil, garlic, ginger, and anise in a container; mix well. Cover and store in refrigerator until use.

3. Remove meat from refrigerator 15 to 20 minutes before grilling. Grill steak and brush ginger glazed on steak.

Potato Beef

This Vietnamese version of meat and potato can be served over rice or eaten alone.

Yield: 6 to 8 servings Prep time: 15 minutes

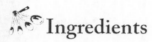

Ingredients

cornstarch	1 1/2 tablespoons
water	1 cup
fish sauce	1 tablespoon
salt	1/2 teaspoon
red potatoes, peeled, sliced 1/4" round shape	2 small
eye of round beef, thinly sliced	2 pounds
onion, cut into wedges	1 medium
garlic, minced	3 cloves
green onion, sliced	2 tablespoons
tomato, cut into 8 wedges	1 medium
canola oil for frying	

Directions:

1. Stir cornstarch, water, fish sauce, and salt in a small bowl until cornstarch is dissolved. Set aside.

2. In a wok, heat about 1/4 cup of canola oil over medium-high heat. Fry potato until golden brown. Remove potato to a plate lined with paper towel. Discard the oil leaving about 2 tablespoons oil in the wok.

3. Stir-fry in the garlic, onion, in the hot oil over high heat for about 30 seconds. Add beef and stir-fry until beef is slightly pink, about 4 to 6 minutes. Add green onion, tomatoes, and continue to stir-fry for another 2 minutes. Push the meat and onion to the side of the wok. Pour the cornstarch mixture to the center of wok, cook and stir until sauce is slightly thickened.

4. Gently toss in fried potatoes with meat and sauce until just combined. Remove from heat and serve.

Beef and bok choy. Replace the fry potato for 2 to 3 bok choy stalks with leaves. Cut cross-wise into bite sizes. Add bok choy to the beef before the scallion and tomatoes. Stir-fry briefly, about 1 minute. Continue as above with adding scallion and tomatoes.

Beef and Spinach Lasagna

Yield: 12 servings Prep time: 20-25 minutes

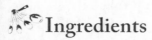

Ingredients

lasagna noodles (tinkyada)	1 box (12 noodles)
lean ground beef	1 pound
onion, chopped	1/4 cup
garlic powder	1 teaspoon
frozen spinach, thawed and drained	1 10-ounce package
pasta sauce, divided	3 cups
Daiya shredded mozzarella cheese	3 cups
mushroom soup (page 95)	1 batch
can coconut milk, light	1 cup
egg, lightly beaten	1 large
tapioca starch	3 tablespoons
salt	1/4 teaspoon
olive oil	1/2 teaspoon

Directions:

1. Preheat oven to 375 degrees F.
2. *For noodles.* Place noodles in boiling water and cook for 2 minutes. Remove from heat and cover for 5 minutes. Rinse noodles in cold water, gently separate and hang noodles to the sides of colander or lay noodles on a baking sheet.
3. Brown beef in a medium skillet over high heat until no longer pink. Drain off fat, stir in onion, garlic powder, spinach, and 2 3/4 cups pasta sauce. Remove from heat and set aside.
4. *For cheese sauce.* Stir together 2 1/2 cups mozzarella cheese, creamy mushroom soup, coconut milk, egg, tapioca starch, and salt until combined.

5. Brush olive oil on a glass 9x13 baking pan. Spread the remaining 1/4 cup of pasta sauce into bottom of the pan. Layer as follows: 3 lasagna noodles, 1/2 of the meat sauce, 3 lasagna noodles, 2/3 of the cheese sauce, 3 lasagna noodles, remaining meat sauce, 3 lasagna noodles, the remaining cheese sauce, and sprinkle the remaining 1/2 cup of mozzarella cheese to cover the top of lasagna.

6. Cover the baking dish with foil and bake for 30 minutes. Remove the foil and continue to bake for another 10 minutes, or until cheese is melted. Change oven to broil on high for 2 minutes. Remove from oven and let stand for 15 minutes before serving.

Tips:

- Ground chicken can be substituted for the beef.
- Most lasagna recipes call for 4 to 7 cups of cheese. GFCFSF cheese is expensive. This recipe reduces the amount of cheese, still tastes cheesy, and saves money.
- Store bought GFCFSF soup can be substituted for the mushroom soup.

Prime Rib Roast

This delicious and no-fail recipe has become a part of our family Christmas dinner tradition.

Yield: 7 to 8 servings Prep time: 20 minutes

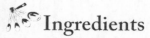

Ingredients

boneless prime rib	5 to 6 pounds
garlic, minced	10 cloves
Cajun spice	2 teaspoons
dried thyme	2 teaspoons
salt	1 1/2 teaspoons
dried rosemary	1 teaspoon
granulated sugar	1/2 teaspoon
onion powder	1/4 teaspoon
paprika	1/4 teaspoon
olive oil	1/4 cup
beef broth	1 1/2 cups

Directions:

1. Clean prime rib and pat dry with paper towel. Poke holes all over the meat with a fork.
2. Stir the garlic, Cajun spice, thyme, salt, rosemary, granulated sugar, onion powder, paprika, and olive oil in a bowl; mix well. Rub the mixture all over meat; wrap the meat tightly in 3 to 4 layers of plastic wraps. Marinade overnight in the refrigerator.
3. Remove prime rib from refrigerator, keep in plastic wrap, to bring meat to room temperature, about 1 1/2 hours before cooking time.
4. Preheat oven to 450 degrees F. Remove plastic wraps, place meat in roasting pan on roasting rack fat side up, roast uncovered for 20 minutes.

5. Turn down oven temperature to 325 degrees F and roast until internal temperature reaches 140 degrees (140 degrees will give medium-rare and more done on end pieces). Every 30 to 45 minutes, baste the roast with liquid accumulated in the roasting pan. Start checking internal temperature about 30 minutes before estimated time. Use 15 minutes per pound to estimate cooking time.

6. Remove roast from oven, cover roast with foil, and let stand for 20 minutes. Internal temperature will continue to rise.

7. While the roast is standing, discard the fat from roasting pan. Place roasting pan over 2 burners on medium heat. Stir in beef broth, salt to taste, and scrape the brown bits. Bring au jus to a boil and cook until stock is reduced to half, about 10 minutes. Filter au jus through a sieve, discard solids, and serve.

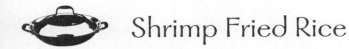

Shrimp Fried Rice

The secret to making great fried rice is the basic ingredients, technique. The meat and vegetables can be replaced with your favorite.

Yield: 4 to 5 servings Prep time: 30 minutes

Ingredients

cooked brown or white rice	3 to 4 cup
olive oil, divided	3 tablespoons
onion, finely chopped	1/4 cup
caramel syrup or mild molasses	1/2 teaspoon
salt	3/4 teaspoon
eggs, lightly beaten	4 large
frozen shrimp, peeled, deveined, and tailed	1/2 pound
frozen diced carrots and peas	1/2 cup
green onion, sliced	3 tablespoons
fish sauce	2 teaspoons

Directions:

1. Place the cold rice in a large bowl, lightly oil your hands and break up the rice clumps. Set aside.
2. Pour 2 tablespoons of olive oil around about an inch from the top of the wok or large skillet and heat oil over high heat. Stir and fry rice for 1 minute.
3. Stir in onion, caramel syrup or molasses, and salt. Stir and fry rice mixture for another 4 to 5 minutes, or until the rice begins to brown. Add a little more oil, 1 teaspoon at a time if the rice is sticking to the bottom of the wok.

4. Push rice to the sides of wok, pour 1 tablespoon olive oil to the center of wok, add eggs to the center of wok; stir continuously until eggs mixture is thick, but not completely cooked. Stir rice and eggs together.
5. Add frozen shrimp, carrots and green peas, green onion, and fish sauce over rice; stir-fry until ingredients are combined and heated through, about 2 minutes.
6. Serve with Seasoned Fish Sauce (page 40) or No-Soy Seasoned Sauce (page 41).

Tips:

- Add 1 tablespoon olive oil when cooking the rice. This will make it easier to work with the rice.
- Cook the rice the day before, refrigerated overnight.
- Fried rice is a great way to use up your leftover meats to reduce preparation time.

Caramelized Shrimp

The authentic method is to leave the shell, tail, and head intact on the shrimp. This sweet, salty, and savory makes it a tasty dish with or without shell.

Yield: 4 servings Prep time: 20 minutes

 ## Ingredients

medium shrimp	1 1/2 pounds
apricot preserves	2 tablespoons
caramel syrup	2 teaspoons
fish sauce	1 tablespoon
salt	1/2 teaspoon
chili flakes	a pinch
olive oil	1 tablespoon
onion, finely chopped	1/4 cup
garlic, minced	3 cloves
green onion, sliced	1 stem

 ## Direction:

1. Place shrimp in a large bowl cover with cold water. Peel, devein, and tailed shrimp. Transfer shrimp to a plate, pat dry, and set aside.
2. Stir together the apricot preserves, caramel syrup, fish sauce, salt, and chili flakes. Set aside.
3. In a wok, heat the olive oil, onion, and garlic over high heat until fragrant. Add shrimp and stir-fry for about 2 minutes or until shrimp is opaque. Transfer shrimp to a plate. Stir in the apricot-mixture, green onion, and stir-fry until sauce is slightly thickened. Add the shrimp to sauce and stir-fry another 2 to 3 minutes. Don't overcook shrimp as they will become rubbery.
4. Remove from heat and serve immediately over rice.

PHOTO
REFERENCE

These photos were all taken in my home kitchen by my husband, Jim. They are not professionally styled. Rather, they are a true reference and depict the results of these recipes.

Asian Bar-B-Que Roast Pork (page 103)

Baked Orange Chicken (page 91)

Asian Bar-B-Que Pork Puffs (page 56)

Brown Rice Buns (page 184)

Pumpkin Pie (page 175)

Caramelized Pork (page 97)

Caramelized Shrimp (page 114)

Egg rolls (page 64), Turkey and Pork Cinnamon Patty (page 62), and Spring rolls (page 43)

Spring Roll sauce, Seasoned Fish sauce, and Peanut sauce

Cherry and Chocolate Chips Scones (page 208)

Chicken Stew (page 75)

Basic Chicken Stir-fry (page 77)

Coconut Cinnamon Bread (page 188)

Coconut Almond Brownie Bites, Peanut Butter Brownie cups, Rocky Road cookies, and Chocolate Chip Cookies

Various Cupcakes and Desserts

Fluffy Blueberry Pancake (page 200)

Shrimp Fried Rice (page 112)

Ginger Glazed Steak (page 105)

Mango Coconut Cream Cobbler (page 170)

Creamy Onion Mushroom Chicken (page 95)

Honey Orange Glazed Chicken (page 85)

Caramelized Pork Pizza (page 58)

Pork and Shrimp Saute Noodle (page 103)

Pork Chops and Tomato Sauce (page 99)

Potato Beef (page 106)

Pot Stickers (page 68)

Pumpkin Cranberry Muffins (page 204)

Chicken Rice Soup (page 74)

Joshua Savory Bites (page 190)

Honey Sesame Chicken (page 79)

Simple Chicken Saute (page 81)

Sweet Rice Stuffed Chicken (page 92)

Chicken Nuggets (page 50) and Turkey Hot Pockets (page 54)

Mini Xiu-Mai Meatball Sub (page 60)

PART 5:
SWEET TREATS...

Sweet treats are items you want to have plenty made ahead and in petite size for ready-to-go any time. One of the benefits with taking control with food is the amount of sweets your child gets.

I've tried to reduce the amount of sugar in most recipes or use agave syrup, which has a lower glycemic index, where possible. For the "really sweet" items, I serve them in smaller portions.

The cookies include small and large batch measurements because they go quick!

Chocolate Chip Cookies

Even our guests' kids and adults that are not on the diet ask for these!

Yield: 30 to 60 cookies Prep time: 20 minutes

Ingredients

Ingredients	Small	Large
JJ Cookie-Base Blend	1 3/4 cups	3 1/2 cups
sweet rice flour	1/4 cup	1/2 cup
xanthan gum	1 teaspoon	2 teaspoons
baking soda	1 teaspoon	2 teaspoons
salt	1/4 teaspoon	1/2 teaspoon
shortening	3/4 cup	1 1/2 cups
creamy peanut butter	1/4 cup	1/2 cup
caramel syrup (optional)	1/4 teaspoon	1/2 teaspoon
granulated sugar	2/3 cup	1 1/3 cups
firmly packed brown sugar	2/3 cup	1 1/3 cups
vanilla extract	1 tablespoon	2 tablespoons
eggs	2 large	4 large
chopped walnuts	1 cup	2 cups
mini semisweet chocolate chips	1 cup	2 cups

Directions:

1. Preheat oven to 350 degrees F. Line baking sheets with parchment paper.
2. Whisk together JJ Cookie-Base Blend, sweet rice flour, xanthum gum, baking soda, and salt in a bowl; mix well and set aside.
3. In a large mixing bowl, beat shortening, peanut butter, caramel syrup, granulated sugar, and brown sugar on medium speed until light and fluffy, about 2 minutes. Add in vanilla extract. Beat in one egg at a time thoroughly before adding the next egg. Add in the flour mixture

and beat on low speed just until dry ingredients are moist, scrape sides of mixing bowl, and beat on medium speed until mixture is blended. Fold in walnuts and chocolate chips.

4. Scoop a heaping tablespoon cookie dough on the prepared baking sheet, 2" apart

5. Bake 9 minutes. Remove from oven. Wait 1 minute, transfer cookies to cooling rack.

Tips:

- Using mini-chocolate chips make cookies look like they have a lot more chips.
- 9 minutes baking makes soft cookies. For crunchier cookies, bake cookies for another 2 minutes.
- Use multiple baking sheets for continuous baking and allowing time for baking sheet to cool.

Rocky Road Cookies

Yield: 30 to 60 cookies Prep time: 25 minutes

Ingredients

Ingredients	Small	Large
JJ Cookie-Base Blend	1 1/2 cups	3 cups
unsweetened cocoa powder	1/2 cup	1 cup
cornstarch	2 tablespoons	1/4 cup
baking powder	2 teaspoons	4 teaspoons
xanthum gum	3/4 teaspoon	1 1/2 teaspoons
baking soda	1/2 teaspoon	1 teaspoon
salt	1/2 teaspoon	1 teaspoon
shortening	2/3 cup	1 1/3 cups
creamy peanut butter	1/3 cup	2/3 cup
granulated sugar	1 cup	2 cup
firmly packed brown sugar	1/2 cup	1 cup
vanilla extract	1 tablespoon	2 tablespoons
eggs	2 large	4 large
chopped walnuts	1/2 cup	1 cup
mini semisweet chocolate chips	1/2 cup	1 cup
mini marshmallows	30	60

Directions:

1. Preheat oven to 350 degrees F. Line baking sheets with parchment paper.
2. Whisk together the JJ Cookie-Base Blend, cocoa powder, cornstarch, baking powder, xanthum gum, baking soda, and salt in a bowl. Mix well and set aside.
3. In a large mixing bowl, beat shortening, peanut butter, granulated sugar, and brown sugar on medium speed until light and fluffy, about 2 minutes. Add in vanilla extract, and beat in one egg at a time thoroughly before adding the next egg. Add in the flour mixture and beat

on low speed just until dry ingredients are moist, scrape sides of mixing bowl, and beat on medium speed until mixture is blended. Fold in walnuts and chocolate chips.

4. Scoop 2 tablespoons cookie dough on prepared baking sheet about 2" apart, press 1 marshmallow to the center of each cookie. Use your hand to shape dough to close the marshmallow in the cookie dough.

5. Bake 9 minutes. Remove from oven. Wait 1 minute, transfer cookies to cooling rack.

Coconut Almond Brownie Bites

These bites are moist, fudgy, and chewy!

Yield: 30 to 60 brownies Prep time: 25 minutes

Ingredients

Ingredients	Small	Large
dried shredded coconut, unsweetened	1/2 cup	1 cup
Quick or Rolled Oats (see page 211)	2 cups	4 cups
JJ Cookie-Base Blend	3/4 cup	1 1/2 cups
unsweetened cocoa powder	1/2 cup	1 cup
xanthum gum	1 teaspoon	2 teaspoons
baking soda	1 teaspoon	2 teaspoons
baking powder	1/2 teaspoon	1 teaspoon
salt	1/4 teaspoon	1/2 teaspoon
coconut oil	3/4 cup	1 1/2 cups
firmly packed brown sugar	1 1/3 cups	2 2/3 cups
eggs	2 large	4 large
can coconut milk	1/4 cup	1/2 cup
vanilla extract	1 teaspoon	2 teaspoons
sliced almonds	1 cup	2 cups
semisweet mini chocolate chips	1/2 cup	1 cup

Directions:

1. Preheat oven to 350 degrees F. Line baking sheets with parchment paper.
2. Fluff dried coconut and 1/4 cup warm water with a fork thoroughly, cover bowl with plastic wrap, and set aside.
3. In a separate bowl, whisk the oats, JJ Cookie-Base Blend, cocoa powder, xanthum gum, baking soda, baking powder, and salt; mix well.

4. In a large mixing bowl, beat coconut oil and brown sugar on medium speed until light and fluffy. Beat in eggs, coconut milk, and vanilla extract until smooth, about 1 minute. Add in the oat-flour mixture and beat on low speed just until dry ingredients are moist, scrape sides of mixing bowl, and beat on medium speed until blended, about 30 seconds. Fold in sliced almonds, chocolate chips, and hydrated coconut.

5. Scoop 2 tablespoons brownie dough on the prepared baking sheet, 2" apart.

6. Bake for 9 to 10 minutes. Remove from oven. Wait 1 minute, transfer brownie bites to cooling rack.

Tips:

- Coconut oil is great way to reduce fat. If you don't have coconut oil, 1 cup of shortening may be substituted for the 3/4 cup coconut oil.

Peanut Butter Brownie Cups

The chocolate peanut butter cups usually make a mess at room temperature. I made this so that it's more convenient for packing on the go!

Yield: 25 cups Prep time: 30 minutes

Ingredients

Coconut Almond Brownie Bites (page 156)	small batch
Filling	
creamy peanut butter	1 cup
confectioner sugar	1/2 cup

Directions:

1. Preheat oven to 350 degrees F. Lightly grease a mini muffin pan with shortening.
2. Prepare Coconut Almond Brownie Bites dough.
3. For filling. Mix the peanut butter and confectioner sugar in a bowl; mix well and set aside.
4. Place 2 tablespoons brownie dough into each mini muffin cup, push the dough with your thumb to make a hole in the center.
5. Bake for 9 to 10 minutes. Remove from oven. Immediately, reshape the center of cups with a wide-end of a chopstick or any stick if necessary. Transfer brownie cups to cooling rack.
6. Once brownie cups are cooled, fill the center with peanut butter filling.

Fudgy Brownies

Yield: 24 2" brownies Prep time: 20 minutes

Ingredients

boiling water	1/2 cup
unsweetened cocoa powder	1 cup
granulated sugar	1 3/4 cups
light olive oil	1/2 cup
vanilla extract	1 teaspoon
JJ Cookie-Base Blend	1 1/4 cups
baking soda	3/4 teaspoon
xanthum gum	1 teaspoon
salt	1/4 teaspoon
eggs	3 large
chopped walnuts	3/4 cup
semisweet chocolate chips (optional)	1/4 cup

Directions:

1. Preheat oven to 350 degrees F. Lightly grease a 9x13 inch pan with shortening.
2. In a small saucepan, heat water to a boil. Remove from heat, stir in cocoa powder, granulated sugar, oil, and vanilla extract.
3. In a large bowl, whisk together the JJ Cookie-Base Blend, baking soda, xanthum gum, and salt. Whisk in the cocoa mixture and eggs until just combined. Batter will be thick.
4. Fold in chopped walnuts and chocolate chips. Spoon batter into the prepared baking pan; use a spreader spatula to smooth batter evenly.
5. Bake 25 minutes, or until a toothpick inserted into the center comes out with just a few moist crumbs clinging to it.

Tips:

- Cut brownies into serving size, wrap each tightly in a plastic wrap, place in a freezer plastic bag, and freeze until use.
- Brownie buster parfait. Break up one brownie serving into small pieces. Place a small scoop of vanilla ice cream in a parfait glass, top with chocolate ganache, another layer of ice cream, half of the brownie pieces and walnuts; repeat with another layer into the glass.

Chocolate Cupcakes

Cupcakes have been our main "to-go" desserts for years, and it's so nice to see how popular it is these days. They are much easier to pack and you can create many desserts with them.

Yield: 18 cupcakes Prep time: 20 minutes

Ingredients

JJ Cake-Base Blend	2 cups
xanthum gum	1 1/2 teaspoons
baking soda	2 teaspoons
baking powder	1 teaspoon
salt	1/2 teaspoon
unsweetened cocoa powder	2/3 cup
hot water	1 1/4 cups
granulated sugar	1 1/2 cups
light olive oil	1 cup
eggs	3 large

Directions:

1. Preheat oven to 350 degrees F. Place paper baking cup in each of regular-size muffin cup pan or lightly grease muffin cups with shortening.
2. In a bowl, whisk together the JJ Cake-Base Blend, xanthum gum, baking soda, baking powder, and salt. Set aside.
3. In another bowl, stir cocoa powder and hot water until cocoa is dissolved. Set aside.
4. In a large mixing bowl, beat granulated sugar, olive oil, and eggs on medium speed until light and lemony texture. On low speed, alternately add flour mixture and cocoa water, scraping bowl occasionally. Beat until just blend.
5. Fill each muffin cups about 2/3 full.

6. Bake 18 to 20 minutes, or until a toothpick inserted in the center comes out clean. Cool in pans for 5 minutes. Transfer cupcakes to cooling racks.

Trip-chocolate cake. Fold 1/2 cup mini-chocolate chips into the batter. Divide batter into 2 8-inch lightly greased cake pans, and bake for 25 minutes or until done. Spread the cooled cakes with chocolate icing. This is a popular birthday cake.

Whoopie pie cake. Stir together 2 tablespoons marshmallow cream, 1/2 tablespoon confectioner sugar, 1/2 tablespoon margarine. Slice cupcake horizontally, spoon marshmallow filling, and place top cupcake over filling.

 Tips:

- Make 2 desserts with 1.
  - Use a small melon scooper or spoon, scoop out the center; fill cupcakes with pudding or icing.
  - Crumble the scooped cupcakes, mix with icing or chocolate ganache to make cake pops.
- Wrap each cupcake tightly in plastic wrap and place in a freezer bag. Store in freezer.

White Cupcakes

Yield: 18 cupcakes Prep time: 15 minutes

Ingredients

JJ Cake-Base Blend	2 1/4 cups
rice flour	1/4 cup
xanthum gum	1 1/2 teaspoons
baking powder	3 teaspoons
baking soda	1 teaspoon
salt	1/2 teaspoon
granulated sugar	1 1/2 cups
eggs	4 large
light olive oil	1 cup
rice milk	1 cup
vanilla extract	1 teaspoon

Directions:

1. Preheat oven to 350 degrees F. Place paper baking cup in each of regular-size muffin cup pan or lightly grease muffin cups with shortening.
2. In a bowl, whisk together the JJ Cake-Base Blend, rice flour, xanthum gum, baking powder, baking soda, and salt. Set aside.
3. In a large mixing bowl, beat granulated sugar, eggs, and olive oil on medium speed until light and lemony texture. On low speed, alternately add flour mixture and rice milk. Add vanilla extract, scraping bowl occasionally and beat until just blended.
4. Fill each muffin cups about 2/3 full.
5. Bake 18 to 20 minutes, or until a toothpick inserted in the center comes out clean. Cool in pans for 5 minutes. Transfer cupcakes to cooling racks.

Pineapple cupcake. Substitute the rice milk for unsweetened pineapple juice.

Banana split cake. Slice cupcake lengthwise into 4 slices, top cake with banana slices, chopped strawberry, and crushed pineapple. Drizzle melted chocolate over cake.

 Tips:

- Fill half of the cupcakes *with* fillings and keep the other half without fillings to make other sweet treats.
- Wrap each cupcake tightly in plastic wrap and place in a freezer bag. Store in freezer.

Soda Cupcakes

Yield: 18 cupcakes Prep time: 15 minutes

Ingredients

JJ Cake-Base Blend	2 1/4 cups
rice flour	1/4 cup
xanthum gum	1 1/2 teaspoons
baking powder	2 teaspoons
baking soda	1 teaspoon
salt	1/2 teaspoon
granulated sugar	1 cup
eggs	4 large
light olive oil	1 cup
favorite flavor carbonated-soda	1 cup

Directions:

1. Preheat oven to 350 degrees F. Place paper baking cup in each of regular-size muffin cup pan or lightly grease muffin cups with shortening.

2. In a bowl, whisk the JJ Cake-Base Blend, rice flour, xanthum gum, baking powder, baking soda, and salt. Set aside.

3. In a large mixing bowl, beat granulated sugar, eggs, and olive oil on medium speed until light and lemony texture. On low speed, alternately add flour mixture and soda, scraping bowl occasionally. Beat until just blended.

4. Fill each muffin cups about 2/3 full.

5. Bake 18 to 20 minutes, or until a toothpick inserted in the center comes out clean. Cool in pans for 5 minutes. Transfer cupcakes to cooling racks.

Tips:

- Soda fountain cake. Slice cupcake in half horizontally, place the top half on a plate, top with a scoop of ice cream, drizzle a small amount of melted chocolate chips, place the bottom half of cupcake over ice cream, top with another scoop of ice cream, melted chocolate chips, and nuts.
- Wrap each cupcake tightly in plastic wrap and place in a freezer bag. Store in freezer.

Lava Cake

This "special treat" is the most frequently requested by the kids and their friends.

Yield: 4 cakes Prep time: 15 minutes

Ingredients

semisweet mini-chocolate chips	3/4 cup
margarine	1/2 cup
confectioner sugar	3/4 cup
eggs	2 large
egg yolks	2 large
JJ Cake-Base Blend	6 tablespoons
xanthum gum	1/8 teaspoon

Directions:

1. Preheat oven to 425 degrees F. Lightly grease 4 ramekins (about 3 1/2 inch diameter).
2. Microwave chocolate chips and margarine in a large microwaveable bowl on high 1 minute, or until margarine melted. Stir with until chocolate is completely melted.
3. Stir in confectioner sugar until well blended. Whisk in eggs and egg yolks until blended, add in JJ Cake-Base Blend and xanthum gum; mix well.
4. Divide and spoon batter into prepared ramekins.
5. Bake 8 to 10 minutes, or until sides are firm and center is soft. Don't over bake. Remove from oven and let stand on wire rack for 5 minutes.
6. Loosen edges of cake, and invert it on to a serving plate. Serve warm.

Coconut Flan

The maple syrup gives a lighter taste than the traditional caramel and reduces preparation time.

Yield: 4 Prep time: 15 minutes

Ingredients

maple syrup	1/2 cup
can coconut milk	1 13.5-ounce
rice milk	1/4 cup
granulated sugar	1/3 cup
eggs	4 large
vanilla extract	1 teaspoon

Directions:

1. Preheat oven to 325 degrees F. Lightly grease 4 ramekins (about 3.5-inch diameter) with margarine.

2. Simmer maple syrup in a small saucepan over medium-high heat until syrup is thickened or registers 260 degrees.

3. Immediately pour the maple syrup in each of the 4 ramekins. Move ramekins around to cover the bottom. Set aside.

4. Stir and cook coconut milk and rice milk in a saucepan over medium heat until bubbles appear around the edge. Remove from heat and whisk in granulated sugar and vanilla extract until sugar is dissolved. Beat in eggs on medium speed for 2 minutes. Gently spoon custard mixture in each ramekin.

5. Place ramekins into a 9x13 glass baking pan and fill water in baking pan until it reaches about 1/2 of the ramekins.

6. Bake 45 to 50 minutes, or until a toothpick inserted into custard comes out clean. The center of custard should wobble just a slightly.

7. Remove from oven and cool ramekins on cooling rack. Cover and store cooled custard in the refrigerator for at least 4 hours before serving.
8. Loosen the edges, and then turn out of the ramekin on to a serving plate.

Chocolate flan. Substitute the rice milk for chocolate rice milk. Stir in 1 tablespoon of unsweetened cocoa powder when heating the milk. Follow above directions.

Mango Coconut Cream Cobbler

Coconut sauce is often used over many Vietnamese desserts, and it's delicious over cobbler.

Yield: 10 servings Prep time: 20 minutes

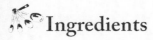 **Ingredients**

Filling

mango in syrup	2 15-ounce cans
tapioca starch	1 tablespoon

Crust

JJ Cake-Base Blend	3/4 cup
brown rice flour	1/4 cup
granulated sugar	1/2 cup
dried shredded coconut, unsweetened	2 tablespoons
baking powder	2 teaspoons
xanthum gum	1/2 teaspoon
cinnamon	1/2 teaspoon
salt	1/4 teaspoon
agave syrup or honey	1 tablespoon
can light coconut milk, divided	3/4 cup
margarine, cold	1/4 cup

Coconut Sauce

can light coconut milk	remaining coconut milk can, about 3/4 cup
tapioca starch	1 teaspoon
granulated sugar	2 tablespoons

Directions:

1. Preheat oven to 375 degrees F.
2. *For filling.* Pour the mango juice in a small bowl. Stir in the 1 tablespoon tapioca starch until starch is dissolved.
3. Place mangoes in a 9x13 glass baking pan and cut mangoes to bite-size pieces. Pour the starch mixture over mangoes.
4. *For crust.* Whisk the JJ Cake-Base Flour Blend, brown rice flour, 1/2 cup granulated sugar, coconut, baking powder, xanthum gum, cinnamon, and salt until combined. Whisk in the 1/2 cup coconut milk, agave or honey; mix well by hand.
5. Pinch small pieces of dough and place it over mango mixture. You could use all or just the amount of dough you like on the cobbler. Cut margarine into small pieces with a butter knife and lay it over the dough. Gently, spoon 1/4 cup coconut milk over dough.
6. Bake for 26 to 28 minutes, or until the crust is golden brown.
7. *For coconut sauce.* Stir the remaining 3/4 cup coconut milk, tapioca starch, and granulated sugar in a saucepan until starch is dissolved. Stir and cook over medium-high heat until sauce is slightly thickened, about 2 minutes.
8. Serve cobbler warm with coconut sauce.

German Chocolate Pie

This recipe came from the Stone Hill Winery restaurant in Missouri. I've modified it for the diet and change the crust to using my Quick Cinnamon Coconut Crust. It was a big hit with our family and friends.

Yield: 1 9" pie Prep time: 25 minutes

 Ingredients

Quick Cinnamon Coconut crust (page 178)	1
semisweet mini-chocolate chips	1/3 cup
margarine	1/2 cup
unsweetened cocoa powder	2 tablespoons
granulated sugar	1 1/4 cups
cornstarch	2 tablespoons
eggs	4 large
vanilla extract	1 teaspoon
can coconut milk	1 14.5-ounce can
dried shredded coconut, unsweetened	2 tablespoons
pecan pieces	2 tablespoons

 Directions:

1. Preheat oven to 350 degrees F.
2. Prepare the Quick Cinnamon Coconut crust, press crust into a glass or ceramic pie pan, and place in the refrigerator while making pie filling.
3. In a saucepan, heat the chocolate chips, margarine, and cocoa powder over medium-low heat until melted. Remove from heat and set aside.
4. In a separate bowl, whisk the granulated sugar and cornstarch together.

5. In a large mixing bowl, beat the eggs with electric mixer on medium speed until foamy and thick. Add in the sugar cornstarch mixture, vanilla extract, chocolate mixture, and beat on medium speed until well incorporated. Fold in the coconut milk until blended.
6. Pour chocolate mixture into the prepared pie crust. Sprinkle with coconut and pecan pieces.
7. Bake for 50 minutes. Remove from oven and cool on wire racks.

Maple Pecan Pie

Yield: 1 9" pie Prep time: 30 minutes

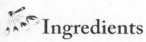

Ingredients

9" pie crust (page 176)	1
maple syrup	1 cup
firmly packed brown sugar	1/3 cup
dark corn syrup	1/3 cup
eggs	3 large
rice flour	3 tablespoons
margarine	2 tablespoons
molasses	1 teaspoon
vanilla extract	1 teaspoon
pecan halves	1 1/4 cups

Directions:

1. Preheat oven to 350 degrees F.
2. Prepare one 9" pie crust, crimp dough edges and set aside.
3. In a bowl, whisk together the maple syrup, brown sugar, corn syrup, eggs, rice flour, margarine, molasses, and vanilla extract until thoroughly mixed. Stir in pecans.
4. Pour pie mixture in the prepared pie dough. Shield dough edges with aluminum foil or pie shield.
5. Bake 45 minutes, or until center is set. The pie is done when the center bounces back when tapped. Cool completely on a wire rack.

# Pumpkin Pie

Yield: 1 9" pie   Prep time: 30 minutes

Ingredients

9" pie crust (page 176)	1
puree pumpkin	1 15-ounce can
can coconut milk, light	1 cup
maple syrup	3/4 cup
eggs	3 large
margarine, melted	1 tablespoon
pumpkin pie spice	1 teaspoon
ground cinnamon	3/4 teaspoon
salt	1/4 teaspoon

## Directions:

1. Preheat the oven to 350 degrees F.
2. In a bowl, whisk together the pumpkin puree, coconut milk, maple syrup, eggs, margarine, pumpkin pie spice, cinnamon, and salt until thoroughly mixed. Set aside.
3. Prepare one 9" pie crust, trim excess crust, crimp dough edges and set aside.
4. Pour pie mixture in the prepared pie dough. Shield dough edges with foil or pie crust shield.
5. Bake 45 to 50 minutes, or until a toothpick inserted comes out moist and clean. Remove from oven and cool on wire rack.

Tips:

- For best flavor, prepare pie filling the night before. Cover and refrigerate overnight.

Pie Crust

Yield: 1 single 9" crust Prep time: 20 minutes

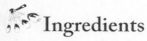 ## Ingredients

JJ Cake-Base Blend	1 2/3 cups
brown rice flour	1/4 cup
brown sugar	1 tablespoon
xanthum gum	1 teaspoon
baking powder	1 teaspoon
salt	1/4 teaspoon
shortening	2/3 cup
margarine, cold	1 tablespoon
egg	1 large
rice vinegar	1/2 tablespoon
iced cold water	1 to 3 tablespoons
rice flour for rolling	

 ## Directions:

1. Lightly grease a 9" glass or ceramic pie pan with shortening.
2. In a large bowl, whisk together the JJ Cake-Base Blend, brown rice flour, brown sugar, xanthum gum, baking powder, and salt. Mix well.
3. Add the shortening, and cold margarine into the flour mixture. Mix by hand until mixture is a crumbly texture, with some pea-sized chunks remaining.
4. Whisk the egg, rice vinegar, and 2 tablespoons cold water until foamy. Add egg mixture to the flour mixture. Mix by hand until the mixture holds together to form a ball, adding 1/2 tablespoon of cold water as necessary.

5. Roll out the dough between 2 layers of plastic wraps that been sprinkle with rice flour. Roll the dough from center to edges, forming a circle 12-13 inches in diameter. Invert the dough into the prepared pie pan.
6. Follow pie recipe direction.

For prebake pie shell recipe: Prepare as above and preheat the oven to 425 degrees F. Prick the dough with a fork on the sides and bottom. Bake 12 to 14 minutes, until the crust is golden.

Tips:

- A food processor does a great job with mixing pie dough and quicker than by hand.

Quick Cinnamon Coconut Crust

This simple crumb crust has gotten many compliments.

Yield: single crust Prep time: 10 minutes

Ingredients

JJ Crumbs-Base Blend	1 1/2 cups
brown sugar	2 tablespoons
ground cinnamon	1 1/2 teaspoons
margarine	1/2 cup

Directions:

1. Lightly grease a 9" pie pan with shortening.
2. In a medium bowl, whisk together the JJ Crumbs-Base Blend, brown sugar, and cinnamon; mix well. Cut in the cold margarine and mix by hand until mixture is thoroughly combined.
3. Press the crumb mixture onto a 9" pie pan.
4. Follow pie recipe direction.

Simple Vanilla Ice Cream

Homemade ice cream is very simple and quick to make and costs less than store bought ice cream.

Yield: 8 1/2-cup Prep time: 10 minutes

Ingredients

can coconut milk	1 13.5-ounce can
rice milk	1 1/4 cups
granulated sugar	3/4 cup
Vance DariFree milk powder	2 tablespoons
caramel syrup	1 teaspoon
margarine	2 tablespoons
vanilla extract	2 teaspoons

Directions:

1. Cook and stir the coconut milk, rice milk, granulated sugar, DariFree milk powder, and caramel syrup in a saucepan over medium heat until mixture is just barely bubble or simmer. Remove from heat, stir in margarine, and vanilla extract; mix well. Cover and store cream mixture in the refrigerator overnight or at least 4 hours.
2. Pour the cold cream mixture in a mixing bowl. Beat the cream mixture on high speed using an electric mixer for about 5 minutes.
3. Pour the whipped cream mixture in the ice cream maker container. Follow manufacturer's directions.
4. Scoop ice cream into individual serving containers with lid. Store in the freezer for at least an hour before serving.

Chocolate chips. Finely grind or chop 2 to 3 tablespoons of semisweet chocolate chips. Add chopped chips the last 5 minutes of the ice cream making time.

Chocolate ice cream. Reduce granulated sugar to 1/3 cup and eliminate the vanilla extract. Stir in 1/2 cup semisweet chocolate chips with the milk-sugar mixture. Follow the recipe direction.

 ## Tips:

- Save money and reuse margarine plastic containers as ice cream cups.

Mango Cream Shake

This is a quick and delicious way to use up your leftover coconut milk.

Yield: 3 1/2 cups Prep time: 5 minutes

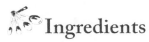

Ingredients

mango juice	1 cup
can coconut milk, light	1 cup
orange juice	1/2 cup
agave syrup or honey	1/3 cup
Vance DariFree milk powder	2 tablespoons
ice cubes	1 cup

Directions:

1. Place mango juice, coconut milk, orange juice, agave syrup, and DariFree milk powder in container of electric blender.
2. Cover and blend on high speed about 20 seconds. Add in ice cubes and blend on high until shake is smooth. Serve cold.

Mango cream pops. Divide shake into a Popsicle tray. Freeze until use.

PART 6:
BREAD

I didn't like the idea of yeast-free bread at first. But I learned to like it a lot because it's much quicker to make than yeast bread.

Buns or mini-baguette shapes are the way to go with gluten, soy, and yeast-free bread. They can serve the same purpose as loaf bread and more. They are easier to store, pack to-go, and easy to turn into many ways to eat bread.

This section includes the basic breads we use for many purposes. I hope you'll find they will work for your family.

Brown Rice Buns

This bread's texture is very close to yeast bread. Brown rice flour gives the best of both worlds, higher in fiber and nutrients than white rice flour, and tastes like white bread.

Yield: 7 to 14 buns Prep time: 25 minutes

Ingredients

Ingredients	Small	Large
rice milk, warm	2/3 cup	1 1/3 cups
rice vinegar	2 teaspoons	4 teaspoons
JJ Cake-Base Blend	1 2/3 cups	3 1/3 cups
brown rice flour	1/3 cup	2/3 cup
brown sugar	3 tablespoons	6 tablespoons
baking powder	1 tablespoon	2 tablespoons
xanthum gum	1 teaspoon	2 teaspoons
salt	1/2 teaspoon	1 teaspoon
baking soda	1/4 teaspoon	1/2 teaspoon
light olive oil	3 tablespoons	6 tablespoons
eggs	2 large	4 large
rice milk, for topping buns		

Directions:

1. Preheat oven to 350 degrees F. Line baking sheet with parchment paper or lightly grease baking sheet with shortening.
2. Stir in rice milk and rice vinegar in a bowl. Set aside.
3. In a large mixing bowl, whisk together the JJ Cake-Base Blend, brown rice flour, brown sugar, baking powder, xanthum gum, salt, and baking soda; mix well.
4. Add in the sour milk and beat on low speed until mixture is just combined. Pour in olive oil and beat on medium speed until blended.

5. Beat in one egg at a time on medium speed before adding the next egg. Scrape the bottom and sides of bowl, and then beat on high speed 2 minutes. Batter should be smooth and thick.

6. Scoop about 1/4 cup of batter on to the prepared baking pan. Spread batter into a round (4" diameter) or mini-baguettes shape using the spreader spatula. Brush rice milk over batter.

7. Bake 20 minutes, or until golden brown. Cover the buns loosely with aluminum foil after 15 minutes of baking.

Sorghum buns. Sorghum bread texture is similar to whole wheat bread and higher in nutrients than brown rice. Replace the 1/3 cup brown rice flour for 1/4 cup sorghum flour; add another 1 teaspoon baking powder, and 1 tablespoon rice milk. Follow the above instructions.

Tips:

- Slice baguette horizontally to make garlic toast, or toasted crostini.
- Slice buns or slice baguette lengthwise to make into pizza bread.
- Save your mistake bread and make them into croutons.
- An easy way to shape mini-baguette is to place batter into a pastry bag, pipe batter into a 4" length, use a spreader to widen the shape.
- For loaf bread, I highly recommend using mini-loaf or 8.5x4.5-inch loaf pan. Follow recipe direction and bake 45 to 48 minutes.
- Wrap each bun or baguette tightly in plastic wrap, place in the freezer storage bag, and freeze until use.

Tapioca Buns

If you prefer white bread, this recipe is closer to the texture and taste of white bread.

Yield: 7 to 14 buns Prep time: 25 minutes

Ingredients	Small	Large
rice milk, warm	1/2 cup	1 cup
rice vinegar	2 teaspoons	4 teaspoons
JJ Cake-Base Blend	1 3/4 cups	3 1/2 cups
tapioca starch	1/4 cup	1/2 cup
brown sugar	3 tablespoons	6 tablespoons
baking powder	1 tablespoon	2 tablespoons
xanthum gum	1 teaspoon	2 teaspoons
salt	1/2 teaspoon	1 teaspoon
baking soda	1/4 teaspoon	1/2 teaspoon
light olive oil	3 tablespoons	6 tablespoons
eggs	2 large	4 large
egg white	1 large	2 large
rice milk, for topping buns		

Directions:

1. Preheat oven to 350 degrees F. Line baking sheet with parchment paper or lightly grease baking sheet with shortening.
2. Stir in rice milk and rice vinegar in a bowl. Set aside.
3. In a large mixing bowl, whisk the JJ Cake-Base Blend, tapioca starch, brown sugar, baking powder, xanthum gum, salt, and baking soda; mix well.
4. Add in the sour milk and beat on low speed until mixture is just combined. Pour in olive oil and beat on medium speed until blended.

5. Beat in one egg and egg white at a time on medium speed before adding the next egg. Scrape the bottom and sides of bowl, and then beat on high speed 2 minutes. Batter should be smooth and thick.

6. Scoop batter on to the prepared baking pan. Spread batter into a round (4" diameter) or mini-baguettes shape using the spreader spatula. Brush rice milk over batter.

7. Bake 20 minutes, or until golden brown. Cover the buns loosely with aluminum foil after 15 minutes of baking. Remove from oven and cool on wire rack.

Garlic bread sticks. Follow the above directions through step 5. Place batter in a pastry bag, pipe batter into a 5-inch long stick, sprinkle garlic powder and brush melted margarine over batter. Bake 15 minutes, or until golden. Remove from oven; lightly brush melted margarine over bread sticks.

For a crispy crust baguette, follow the above instructions through step 5. Beat 1 egg white and 1 tablespoon water in a bowl. Shape batter into a mini-baguette size, brush egg white mixture over batter. Bake as above instructions.

Tips:

- See the tips with the Brown Rice Bun recipe (page 184) for ideas on usage.
- Wrap each bun tightly in plastic wrap, and place in the freezer storage bag. Freeze bread until use.

Coconut Cinnamon Bread

This is a good alternative to the sugary cinnamon buns without giving up the cinnamon taste kids love. This goes well with breakfast or any time snack.

Yield: 2 8.5-inch loaves Prep time: 25 minutes

Ingredients

dried shredded coconut, unsweetened	2 tablespoons
can coconut milk, light	1 1/4 cups
rice vinegar	1 tablespoon
brown sugar	1 1/2 tablespoons
ground cinnamon	1/2 tablespoon
JJ Cake-Base Blend	2 1/2 cups
rice flour	1/2 cup
baking powder	1 tablespoon
xanthum gum	1 1/2 teaspoons
baking soda	1/4 teaspoon
salt	1/4 teaspoon
shortening	1/3 cup
granulated sugar	2/3 cup
eggs	3 large

Directions:

1. Preheat oven to 325 degrees F. Lightly grease the bottom of two 8 1/2" by 4 1/2" loaf pans with shortening.
2. Fluff dried coconut and 1 tablespoon warm water with a fork, and cover bowl with plastic wrap. Set aside.
3. Stir coconut milk and vinegar in a separate bowl. Set aside.

4. Stir brown sugar and ground cinnamon in a separate bowl. Set aside.
5. Whisk the JJ Cake-Base Blend, rice flour, baking powder, xanthum gum, baking soda, and salt.
6. In a large mixing bowl, beat shortening and granulated sugar with an electric mixer on medium speed until light and fluffy. Beat in one egg at a time thoroughly before adding the next egg, scraping the sides of the bowl as needed.
7. Stir in the flour mixture and sour coconut milk, beat on low speed until mixture is just moist. Beat batter on medium speed for 1 minute. The batter should be smooth and thick. Fold in the hydrated coconut.
8. Spoon half the batter into each prepared pans, use spreader spatula to level spread the batter evenly across the pan. Sprinkle half the cinnamon-sugar over batter. Spoon the remaining batter over the cinnamon-sugar, level and smooth out the batter with spatula. Sprinkle with the remaining cinnamon-sugar over batter.
9. Bake 50 to 55 minutes, or until a toothpick inserted near the center comes out clean. Let stand in pans 10 minutes. Remove bread from pans and cool on wire rack completely before slicing.

Tips:

- Wrap each slide tightly in plastic wrap, and place in the freezer storage bag. Freeze bread until use.

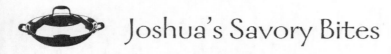

Joshua's Savory Bites

This little tasty savory bites were created for Joshua after we came back from a cruise. The cruise line served a gluten version every night. He was such a trooper and willing wait until we get back home to have his own version.

Yield: 24 bites Prep time: 15 minutes

Ingredients

JJ Cake-Base Blend	1 3/4 cups
brown rice flour	1/4 cup
baking powder	1 tablespoon
xanthum gum	1 teaspoon
garlic salt	1/2 teaspoon
shortening	1/2 cup
margarine, cold	1 tablespoon
rice milk	3/4 cup
eggs, lightly beaten	1 large
agave syrup or honey	2 teaspoons
Daiya shredded cheddar cheese	1/4 cup
dried parsley	1 teaspoon
margarine, melted	2 teaspoons

Directions:

1. Preheat oven to 375 degrees F. Line baking sheet with parchment paper or lightly grease a baking sheet with shortening.
2. In a large mixing bowl, whisk the JJ Cake-Base Blend, brown rice flour, baking powder, xanthum gum, and garlic salt.

3. Add shortening and cold margarine to flour mixture, mix by hand until mixture resembles coarse crumbs.

4. Whisk in the rice milk, egg, agave syrup, cheddar cheese, and parsley until dough is just combined.

5. Drop a heaping tablespoon onto the prepared baking sheet. Bake 10 minutes, or until golden.

6. Remove from oven, lightly brush melted margarine over savory bites, and cool on wire rack. Serve warm.

Tips:

- For quicker preparation, use a food processor to mix the dough.
- For quicker method, replace shortening and 1 tablespoon of margarine with 1/2 cup light olive oil. The savory bites will be a little mealier but still taste good.

Pastry Crust

This is my 'All-purpose' crust. It works great with savory pockets, sweet turnovers, and pizza.

Yield: 25 4-inch length pockets Prep time: 25 minutes

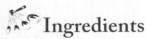

Ingredients

warm water	1 1/4 cups
light olive oil	1/4 cup
rice vinegar	2 teaspoons
agave syrup or honey	1 tablespoon
JJ Cake-Base Blend	3 cups
brown rice flour	1/2 cup
baking powder	2 tablespoons
granulated sugar	1 tablespoon
xanthum gum	2 teaspoons
salt	3/4 teaspoon
egg, lightly beaten	1 large

Directions:

1. Stir warm water, olive oil, rice vinegar, and agave syrup or honey in a bowl. Set aside.

2. In a large mixing bowl, whisk the JJ Cake-Base Blend, brown rice flour, baking powder, granulated sugar, xanthum gum, and salt; mix well.

3. Make a well in the center of the flour mixture; add in water-oil mixture. Using an electric mixer and a hook attachment, mix on low speed until mixture is moist. Beat in egg on high speed until dough is formed and pliable, about 2 minutes. If dough is too dry, add 1 tablespoon of water at a time until desire consistency is reached.

4. Work with dough on a surface cover with rice flour or oil your hand, shape dough as desired, and follow recipe direction.

Thin pizza crust. Preheat oven to 375 degrees F. Prepare pastry dough as directed. Lightly oil your hands, pinch about 3 tablespoons of dough, form into a ball, and press dough onto the prepared baking sheet to form a 6-inch circle or square shape. Repeat with remaining dough. Top dough with your favorite sauce and toppings. Bake 16 to 18 minutes, or until crust edge is golden.

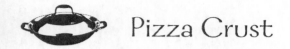

Pizza Crust

This is a thicker pizza crust.

Yield: 12 6-inch crusts Prep time: 15 minutes

Ingredients

warm water	1 1/4 cups
light olive oil	1/3 cup
agave syrup or honey	1 1/2 tablespoons
rice vinegar	1 tablespoon
JJ Cake-Base Blend	3 cups
brown rice flour	1/2 cup
baking powder	2 tablespoons
xanthum gum	1/2 tablespoon
garlic salt	1/2 tablespoon
eggs	2 large

Directions:

1. Preheat oven to 375 degrees F. Line baking sheet with parchment paper or lightly grease with shortening.
2. Stir water, olive oil, agave syrup or honey, and rice vinegar in a bowl. Set aside.
3. In a large mixing bowl, whisk the JJ Cake-Base Blend, brown rice flour, baking powder, xanthum gum, and garlic salt.
4. Make a well in the center of the flour mixture; add the water-oil mixture. Using an electric mixer, mix on low speed until mixture is moist. Beat in one egg at a time on medium speed thoroughly before adding the next egg. Scrape the bottom and sides of bowl, and beat on high speed for about 2 minutes. Batter should be smooth and thick.

5. Scoop about 3 tablespoons of batter onto the prepared baking pan. Spread batter to a flat round or square shape using a spreader spatula.

6. Top batter with your favorite pizza sauce and toppings. Bake 16 to 18 minutes, or until crust is golden.

PART 7:
BREAKFAST

Coconut Sweet Rice (Xoi Vo)

I was so surprised how much the boys liked this authentic breakfast food when my mom made it for them for our trip home. They've asked for it ever since. They call it "Grandma Pho Xoi."

Yield: 6 to 8 servings Prep time: 30 minutes

Ingredients

sweet glutinous rice	3 cups
dried split mung beans	1 cup
dried shredded coconut, unsweetened	1/2 cup
light olive oil	3 tablespoons
salt	1 teaspoon
granulated sugar	3 tablespoons

Directions:

1. Rinse the sweet rice a few times to remove some starches. Soak rice in cold water at room temperature overnight.

2. Rinse mung beans a few times to remove the yellow water. Soak mung beans in a separate bowl with lukewarm water at room temperature overnight.

3. Next day. Steam the mung beans about 20 minutes over medium-high heat.

4. Drain sweet rice in a colander. Set aside.

5. Fluff dried coconut and 1/4 cup warm water with a fork, and cover bowl with plastic wrap. Set aside.

6. Let mung beans stand 10 minutes to cool. Place mung beans in a bowl of a food processor and process mung beans to a fine paste.

7. In a large bowl, place sweet rice, bean paste, shredded coconut, olive oil, and salt. Mix by hand until mixture is incorporated.

8. Place the sweet rice mixture on the top steamer pan. Cover and steam 10 minutes over high heat. Reduce heat to medium-high, and continue to steam another 15 to 18 minutes, or until the rice is cooked.

9. Spread the cooked sweet rice (xoi) on a baking sheet. Stir in granulated sugar. Let stand to cool. Serve warm.

Tips:

- If your steamer pan has large holes, line the top pan with 2 layers of dampened cheesecloth before placing the sweet rice mixture in pan.
- Divide the remaining sweet rice into individual serving sizes, place each serving in a sandwich resealable plastic storage bag, and place the sandwich bags in a freezer storage plastic bag. Store in freezer until use.

# Fluffy Blueberry Pancake

Yield: 12 to 14 servings Prep time: 15 minutes

Ingredients

rice milk	1 1/4 cups
rice vinegar	1 tablespoon
JJ Cake-Base Blend	2 cups
brown rice flour	1/2 cup
baking powder	2 teaspoons
baking soda	1 teaspoon
xanthum gum	1/2 teaspoon
salt	1/4 teaspoon
light olive oil	1/4 cup
eggs	4 large
maple syrup	2 tablespoons
frozen blueberries	1/2 cup

Directions:

1. Stir rice milk and vinegar in a bowl. Set aside.
2. In large mixing bowl, whisk JJ Cake-Base Blend, brown rice flour, baking powder, baking soda, xanthum gum, and salt until combined.
3. Making a well in the center of the flour mixture, add olive oil, sour milk, eggs, and maple syrup. Beat on low speed with an electric mixer until mixture is moist. Beat batter on medium speed for 1 minute. Batter should be smooth and thick. Fold in the blueberries.

Chocolate chip pancakes. Replace the 1/2 cup blueberries for 1/4 cup mini semisweet chocolate chips.

Tips:

- Plain pancakes make great flat bread to make breakfast sausage sandwich, just leave out the blueberries.
- Place pancakes in a freezer plastic bag, and freeze until use.

Peanut Butter and Jam Muffin

I've got this idea from the 2007 *Cooking Light* magazine, modified the recipe, and the boys loved it since.

Yield: 12 muffins Prep time: 20 minutes

 Ingredients

JJ Cake-Base Blend	1 1/4 cups
brown rice flour	1/2 cup
firmly packed brown sugar	1/3 cup
granulated sugar	1/4 cup
baking powder	4 teaspoons
xanthum gum	1 teaspoon
salt	1/4 teaspoon
rice milk	1 1/4 cups
creamy peanut butter	1/3 cup
egg	1 large
light olive oil	3 tablespoons
vanilla extract	1 teaspoon
strawberry preserves	1/4 cup

 Directions:

1. Preheat oven 375 degrees F. Place paper baking up in a regular-size muffin pan or lightly grease muffin pan.

2. Whisk together the JJ Cake-Base Blend, brown rice flour, brown sugar, granulated sugar, baking powder, xanthum gum, and salt; mix well.

3. In a large bowl, whisk the rice milk, peanut butter, egg, oil, and vanilla extract until blended. Whisk in the flour mixture; mix well.

4. Fill each cup half full with batter, spoon 1 teaspoon strawberry preserves in the center of each cup. Top the preserve with the remaining batter.

5. Bake 15 to 17 minutes, or until golden brown. Transfer muffins to wire rack to cool.

PB-chocolate chip muffins. Replace strawberry preserves with 1/3 cup of mini chocolate chips. Fold in chocolate chips after mixing the batter.

Tips:

- Wrap each muffin with tight plastic wrap, place them in a freezer plastic bag, and freeze until use.

Pumpkin Cranberry Muffins

Yield: 24 muffins Prep time: 15 minutes

Ingredients

JJ Cake-Base Blend	2 cups
rice flour	1 cup
baking powder	4 teaspoons
pumpkin spice	3 teaspoons
baking soda	2 teaspoons
xanthum gum	1 teaspoon
salt	1/2 teaspoon
granulated sugar	2/3 cup
pumpkin puree	1 15-ounce can
can coconut milk, light	1 1/3 cups
light olive oil	1/4 cup
eggs	4 large
dried cranberries	1/4 cup
chopped pecans	1/4 cup
granulated sugar (optional), for topping	2 tablespoons

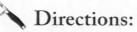

Directions:

1. Preheat oven 375 degrees F. Place paper baking cups in a regular-size muffin pan. Lightly brush cups with shortening.

2. Whisk the JJ Cake-Base Blend, rice flour, baking powder, pumpkin spice, baking soda, xanthum gum, and salt until combined. Set aside.

3. In a large mixing bowl, beat granulated sugar, pumpkin puree, coconut milk, olive oil, and eggs with an electric mixer on medium speed for 1 minute, or until blended.

4. Beat in flour mixture on low speed just until moist. Beat batter on medium speed until batter is just blend. Fold in cranberries and pecans.

5. Fill each cup about 2/3 full. Sprinkle granulated sugar over batter.

6. Bake muffins 18 to 20 minutes, or until toothpick inserted in the center comes out clean or just a few moist crumbs. Transfer muffins to wire rack to cool.

Tips:

- Wrap each muffin in tight plastic wrap, place them in a freezer plastic bag, and freeze until use.

Blueberry Coffee Cake

Yield: 10 servings Prep time: 30 minutes

Ingredients

Filling

brown sugar	3 tablespoons
ground cinnamon	2 teaspoons
pecan pieces	1/2 cup

Batter

JJ Cake-Base Blend	2 1/3 cups
rice flour	1/3 cup
baking powder	1 1/2 tablespoons
xanthum gum	1 teaspoon
salt	1/4 teaspoon
granulated sugar	1/2 cup
margarine	1/4 cup
eggs	3 large
can coconut milk, light	1/4 cup
plain coconut yogurt	1 6-ounce
vanilla extract	2 teaspoons
frozen blueberries, don't thaw	1 cup

Directions:

1. Preheat oven 350 degrees F. Lightly grease a 9x13 glass or ceramic baking pan or a bundt pan.
2. *For filling.* Stir together the brown sugar, cinnamon, and pecans. Set aside.

3. *For batter*. In a separate bowl, whisk together the JJ Cake-Base Blend, rice flour, baking powder, xanthum gum, and salt. Set aside.

4. In a large mixing bowl, beat granulated sugar and margarine with an electric mixer on medium speed until light and fluffy. Beat in one egg at a time thoroughly before adding the next egg. On low speed, beat in the flour mixture, coconut milk, yogurt, and vanilla extract just until batter is blended. Batter should be smooth and thick. Fold in frozen blueberries.

5. Spoon about half of the batter into the prepared baking pan; sprinkle half of the filling over batter. Spoon the remaining batter over the fillings, and top batter with the remaining filling. Use a butter knife to swirl the mixture into the cake.

6. Bake 35 to 40 minutes, or until toothpick inserted in the center comes out clean. Let stand in pan 10 minutes. Remove cake from pan and cool on wire rack.

Blueberry muffins. Eliminate the filling ingredients and directions. Place paper baking cups in regular-size muffin pan. Prepare batter as directed and bake 18 to 20 minutes, or until a toothpick inserted in the center comes out clean.

Cherry and Chocolate Chips Scones

Yield: 14 scones Prep time: 20 minutes

Ingredients

JJ Cake-Base Blend	2 2/3 cups
brown rice flour	1/3 cup
brown sugar, firmly packed	1/3 cup
baking powder	2 tablespoons
xanthum gum	1 1/2 teaspoons
salt	1/4 teaspoon
margarine	1/3 cup
shortening	1/3 cup
eggs, lightly beaten	4 large
can coconut milk, light	1/3 cup
dried cherry, coarsely chopped	1/2 cup
semisweet mini-chocolate chips	1/3 cup
margarine, melted	2 teaspoons
granulated sugar, for topping	2 teaspoons

Directions:

1. Preheat oven to 375 degrees F. Line baking sheet with parchment paper or lightly grease the baking sheet with shortening.
2. In a large mixing bowl, whisk the JJ Cake-Base Blend, brown rice flour, brown sugar, baking powder, xanthum gum, and salt. Cut in the 1/3 cup cold margarine and shortening. Mix by hand until the flour mixture resembles coarse crumbs.
3. Beat in eggs and coconut milk with an electric mixer on low speed until mixture is just combined. Beat dough on medium speed for 30 seconds. Dough should be moist, thick, and pliable. Fold in the cherry and chocolate chips.

4. Scoop about 1/4 cup dough onto the prepared baking pan using a #16 scoop. Flatten the top of dough with your hand, brush melted margarine over dough, and sprinkle with sugar.

5. Bake 11 minutes, or until a toothpick inserted in the center comes out clean. Cool on a wire rack.

Blueberry scones. Replace the dried cherry and chocolate chips with 1 cup frozen blueberries, increase granulated sugar to 1/2 cup. Follow above directions.

Tips:

- Dried cranberry can be substituted for dried cherry.
- Wrap each scone in tight plastic wrap, place them in a freezer plastic bag, and freeze until use.

Almond-Chocolate Spread

This is our mock version of Nutella. The boys consider it a treat with breakfast.

Yield: 2 1/4 cups Prep time: 10 minutes

Ingredients

almond butter	2 cups
confectioner sugar	2/3 cup
unsweetened cocoa powder	1/3 cup
Vance DariFree milk powder	2 tablespoons
agave syrup or honey	3 tablespoons
semisweet chocolate chips, melted	3 tablespoons

Directions:

1. Place all ingredients in the bowl of food processor. Cover and process about 20 seconds, or until mixture is thoroughly combined.

2. Store in an airtight container in the refrigerator until use.

3. To serve. Stir together 1 tablespoon of chocolate spread, and 1 teaspoon rice milk in a bowl until mixture is smooth. Spread over toast or crackers. This method gives the spread a longer shelf life.

SPECIAL HELPERS

Knowing the appropriate food for the diet is a very important first step of this diet. This section contains various helpers to help you with the "need to know" ingredients and various helpful cooking solutions.

COMMON GLUTEN AND SOY FREE (GFSF) FLOURS

CORNSTARCH: This refined starch from corn is mostly used as a thickener. If you are allergic to corn, the rice flour, sweet rice flour, or tapioca are alternatives to cornstarch to thicken sauces.

POTATO STARCH: This is a mild and light starch made from potatoes, and it's commonly used in many gluten-free flour mixes. This starch is very different from potato flour, which is a much heavier texture. This can be found in most large grocery store chains and Asian markets. It will store well in your pantry.

WHITE RICE FLOUR: This is a very common staple for the Vietnamese culture. It is commonly used as a basic for many gluten-free mixes. This can be found in most large grocery store chains and Asian markets. It will store well in your pantry and has a long shelf life.

BROWN RICE FLOUR: Brown rice flour has higher fiber content and other nutritional value than white rice flour. It has slightly nutty taste, but much milder than the bean flours. I store it in the refrigerator for longer shelf life.

OATS: This ingredient is highly controversial with the diet due to cross-contamination with common gluten products. We avoided using oats for years until the "certified gluten-free oats" became available in the market. There is one recipe in the book that uses oats. If you would like to include oats in your diet, start with small quantities and observe for at least a week for adverse effects.

SWEET RICE FLOUR: This flour is made from glutinous rice known as "sticky rice" and is often used in many Vietnamese desserts. It has high starch content and works well as a thickener. Sweet rice flour can be found in Asian markets or online from several suppliers. It will store well in your pantry.

SORGHUM FLOUR (ALSO KNOWN AS SWEET SORGHUM OR JOWAR): Sorghum has a slightly higher fiber and protein contents than brown rice flour. It's the only bean flour I use in recipes because it has a milder taste than other bean flours. It can be found in many large grocery chains. I store it in the refrigerator for longer shelf life.

TAPIOCA STARCH: Tapioca starch is made from the root of cassava plant and often is used in Vietnamese desserts and thickening sauce. It also helps lighten the texture in baked goods. This can be found in most large grocery store chains, Asian markets, or online. It will store well in your pantry.

XANTHAN GUM: Xanthum gum is a corn-based product. It is a key binding ingredient with baking gluten-free. It gives baked products the elasticity and keeps them from crumbling. Guar gum (check with manufacturer for hidden soy) can be used as an alternative if you are sensitive to corn. Be careful measuring this as too much can give your baked goods a heavy texture.

Other GFSF flours. The following is a list of other GFSF flours available in the market place and helpful links when you're ready to try them.

- Arrowroot
- Corn Flour
- Coconut Flour
- Chestnut Flour
- Corn Meal
- Garbanzo Bean Flour
- Garfava Flour

- Guar Gum
- Millet
- Nut Flours
- Potato Flour
- Quinoa
- Teff

Helpful links that contain additional information on the above flours:
http://glutenfreecooking.about.com/od/glutenfreeingredients
www.livingwithout.com

COMMON INGREDIENTS FOR THE VIETNAMESE RECIPES

The Asian market is great place to find alternative ingredients for the diet. However, you need to be careful with your selection as the labeling requirement is questionable. The following are common products used in the book. They can be found in many Asian markets, large grocery chains, and online ordering.

CELLOPHANE NOODLES (BEAN THREADS): These are very thin, dried strand noodles made from mung beans. They are also known as bean threads. Once cooked, the noodle has a translucent, glassy appearance. They usually come in 3.5-ounce to 8-ounce packages.

CHILIES: These tiny green and red peppers are very popular in Vietnamese and Thai cooking. They are very spicy, so use sparingly. These can be stored in the freezer for longer shelf life.

CANNED COCONUT MILK: Canned coconut milk is unsweetened and often used in Vietnamese desserts and has become popular with this diet. It usually comes in a 13.5-ounce can with cream and light options. You'll need to stir or whisk the milk before using as the coconut cream usually separates in the can. An open can of coconut milk will keep in the refrigerator for about 3 to 4 days.

DRIED BLACK MUSHROOMS: These are dried shiitake mushrooms. They must be soaked in water before use. They come in plastic packages and are found in most Asian markets.

DRIED CHILIES: Dried red chilies, whole or in flakes, are a perfectly good substitute for fresh chilies.

FISH SAUCE (NUOC MAM): This is the primary sauce for many Vietnamese dishes. It's a salty amber liquid made from fermented anchovies, which is rich in vitamin B and other nutrients. There are two ways to use this. First, the concentrated sauce from the bottle is used to season food during cooking. A second way is to mix it into a "seasoned sauce" for dipping or additional seasoning to your cooked food similar to soy sauce. Many store-bought premade seasoned fish sauce contains gluten ingredients. Be sure to check the ingredient label.

FIVE-SPICE POWDER: There are various version of the commercial five-spice powder. The taste may be slightly varied depending on the brand you purchase. It's easy to mix your own.

HERBS: Fresh herbs are often used as a side for many of the Asian dishes in the book. The most common are mint leaves, basil, and chives. They provide the same essential nutrients found in other leafy green vegetables.

JICAMA: Jicama is just as popular an Asian vegetable as a Mexican vegetable. It has a crunch and slightly sweet taste. It's best when bought in season and used quickly after purchase as it doesn't last long.

RICE NOODLES: Most Vietnamese noodles are made from rice flour and water. They usually come dried and in a 12- to 14-ounce package. There are varieties of forms—pho noodle is flat and long; bun noodle is a round with small to extra-wide size.

RICE PAPER WRAPPER: Rice paper is the Vietnamese version of tortilla. It's often used as a wrap for eggrolls and spring rolls. They come in a dry form with various size and shapes and have a chewy/stretchy feel after being moistened with water. The traditional way this is made is with rice or tapioca starch. I've recently noticed that some rice paper products now have wheat flour. So be sure to check the ingredient label.

SESAME OIL: This oil, pressed from dark brown sesame seeds, is used sparingly to add a hint of nutty taste. Store sesame oil the refrigerator to keep it fresh.

SHALLOTS: Shallots are used in marinades and toppings with savory dishes. They can be found in the vegetables section in most grocery chains.

STAR ANISE: Star anise is a common Asian spice. They are available in ground, seeds, and whole star-pod forms. The seeds are available in most large grocery chains. The whole star-pods and ground forms can be found in an Asian market or a spice shop.

YELLOW MUNG BEAN: These are peeled and split, dried green mung beans. They are often used as fillings in dessert or over sweet rice. They usually come in a 12-ounce clear package, called yellow mung bean or peeled split mung bean.

For your convenience, the "Printout" section includes common food label ingredients and hidden ingredients guidelines. The printout will easily fit into your wallet, so you'll have them with you all the time.

SUBSTITUTION PRINCIPLES

As you get more experience with this diet, you'll learn many different ways to substitute ingredients. These are the substituting principles I often use that I hope will help you with your own recipes.

GLUTEN SUBSTITUTE

If you are just starting on the diet, I encourage you to stay with basic flour blend and choose less expensive flour until you're more comfortable with baking GF.

For 1 cup of all-purpose flour in your recipe:

- Substitute 3/4 cup of the JJ Cake-Base or JJ Cookie-Base Blend, depending the items you're making (see page 30 and 31). Add 1/4 cup of a second gluten-free flour such as brown rice flour, sorghum, or other GFSF flours. Add 1/2 teaspoon xanthum gum or guargum; mix well.
- The above substitution is a general guideline. The second flour provides a way for you to adjust the texture of the result such as higher fiber, chewy, cakey, etc. You can adjust the ratio between the Base Blend and the second flour to achieve desired texture.
- Each flour absorbs liquid differently. It may be necessary to adjust the liquid amount in the recipe. I usually reserve 1/4 cup of the liquid amount called for in the recipes, observe the texture and consistency, and add the reserved liquid one tablespoon at a time until desired consistency is reached.

CASEIN SUBSTITUTE

Milk substitute. There are many milk options. To keep things simple, I mainly use rice milk or coconut milk. I am glad to see that coconut milk is becoming more common in many gluten-free/casein-free recipes today. The rice milk is used mostly for drinking, eating cereal, and in recipes with a thinner consistency. This includes pancakes and waffles. I use coconut milk for flavoring or recipes need a little more fat such as ice cream, custard, or pudding.

- For 1 cup *cow's milk*, substitute with 1 cup of rice milk or 1 cup coconut milk.
- For 1 cup *buttermilk* or sour milk, substitute with 1 cup of rice milk or coconut milk plus 1 tablespoon of rice vinegar. I adjust the vinegar if the result is too tart.
- For 1 cup *yogurt*, substitute with 1 cup coconut yogurt
- For 1 cup *sour cream*, substitute with 1 cup coconut yogurt, or 1/2 cup plain hummus plus 1/2 cup coconut milk. You can adjust the ratio depending on the recipe's consistency. This works well for substituting cream cheese in some recipes, but not cheesecake.
- For 1 cup *butter*, substitute with:
  - 1 cup Spectrum Organic shortening
  - 1/2 cup Earth Balance GFCFSF spread plus 1/2 cup Spectrum Organic shortening. You may need to adjust the salt measurement in the recipe as this spread contains salt.
  - 7/8 cup light olive or canola oil plus 1 tablespoon of another liquid calls for in the recipe.

Cheese substitution is generally 1 cup for 1 cup GFCFSF Daiya cheese. It wasn't until recently that Daiya cheese came out and I was able to add cheese back to our diet. Daiya brand cheese is the best cheese alternative I've tried. The only downside is the price. So rather than substituting all the cheese called for in a recipe, I use my creamy sauce plus Daiya cheese to make up 1 cup. See the Lasagna recipe for an example. You can adjust the cream sauce-and-cheese ratio depending on your preference. Using smaller amount helps keep the cost down and still get the stretchy ad gooey texture the kids like.

SOY SUBSTITUTE

For soy sauce:

- To season cooked food or dipping, try my No-Soy Seasoned Sauce or the Seasoned Fish Sauce.
- For cooking, I typically add 1/2 teaspoon caramel syrup or mild molasses along with the other spices, seasoning in the recipe. My Asian recipes in the book are examples of ways I use to create flavor and coloring. They are delicious and soy-free.

The *Living Without* magazine and the nonprofit organization Talk About Curing Autism (TACA) are great resources on the diet ingredients and substitutions.

FREQUENTLY USED EQUIPMENT

I used to buy all kinds of kitchen gadgets. Since we transitioned to this diet, I focus buying kitchen equipments on two goals—reduce time or cost. The following are items that made the list I hope will do the same for you.

1. *Stand mixer.* It took me a while to make this investment, and I was really glad afterward. It made the whole mixing process simpler and reduced prep time, especially with larger batches.

2. *Electric ice cream maker.* Store-bought GFCFSF ice cream costs 3 to 4 times more than regular ice cream. This little helper will save you money and simplify ice cream making. Look for my Simple Homemade Ice Cream recipes.

3. *Wok.* A wok can stir-fry food much better than a skillet and easier with big batch.

4. *Food processor.* My mom introduced me to this. It grinds meat and cereal fast and does a great job with mixing pie dough.

5. *Electric rice cooker.* This is a much easier way to make rice. Just add rice and water, and it does the rest.

6. *Airtight containers* to store your flours.

7. *Silicone pad and rolling pin.* If you plan to make pastry, these silicon equipments will make the process a lot simpler for you and requiring less flour during rolling.

8. *Multiple baking sheets*, preferably not nonstick. With multiple baking sheets, you can continue to cook, rotate to allow time for pan to cool, and less chance of over baking.

9. *Scoops.* These help you make consistent sizes for cookies, cupcakes, and bread. I primarily use two scoop sizes: #60—1 tablespoon, and #16 scoop—1/4 cup.

10. *Re-use your plastic containers* and save. Store-bought items such as yogurt and margarine come in small size containers that are perfect for storing single servings of ice cream and chicken stock. Ask your relatives and friends to save these contains for you. My mother-in-law, Peggy, gave me all the plastic containers I need.

One last tip I have for you is this: let go of your preconceived notions and expectations when it comes to "normal food."

Have fun and don't be afraid to try new flavor combinations from multiple cuisines. Don't be afraid of making mistakes; some of my best creations were born from mistakes.

On a final note, I hope you find the base methods, recipes, and tips helpful as you create a new lifestyle for you and your family. I wish you well on your journey!

REFERENCES

Below are organizations and websites I found very helpful and informative with science and latest information on autism.

ANDI Autism Network for Dietary Intervention. www.autismndi.com

National Autism Association (provides great details on the science and discoveries associated with Autism.) www.nationalautismassociation.org

The GFCF Diet Support Group www.gfcfdiet.com

TACA Now. This site has a lot of great articles, a start-up guide to the diet, and in-depth information on financial aid. www.tacanow.org

Autism Speaks. This is a great resource to help you stay on top of latest research, family services, and local clinics. www.autismspeaks.org

RECOMMENDED BOOKS:

Special Diet for Special Child by Lisa Lewis
Gluten-Free Gourmet by Bette Hagman
Living Without Magazine

METRIC CONVERSION CHART

Volume

Cup	Fluid Ounces	Tablespoons	Teaspoons	Milliliters
1 cup	8 oz	16 tbsp	48 tsp	237 ml
3/4 cup	6 oz	12 tbsp	36 tsp	177 ml
2/3 cup	5 oz	11 tbsp	32 tsp	158 ml
1/2 cup	4 oz	8 tbsp	24 tsp	118 ml
1/3 cup	3 oz	5 tbsp	16 tsp	79 ml
1/4 cup	2 oz	4 tbsp	12 tsp	59 ml
1/8 cup	1 oz	2 tbsp	6 tsp	30 ml
1/16 cup	1/2 oz	1 tbsp	3 tsp	15 ml

Temperatures

Fahrenheit	Celsius
300°	150°
325°	160°
350°	180°
375°	190°
400°	200°
425°	220°
450°	230°
475°	240°

PRINTABLES

JJ BLEND RECIPE LABELS

Cut and tape these recipe labels on your flour blend containers.

JJ Cake-Base Blend	
Small	**Large**
2 Cups Rice Flour	4 Cups Rice Flour
3/4 Cup Tapioca Starch	1 1/2 Cups Tapioca Starch
3/4 Cup Potato Starch	1 1/2 Cups Potato Starch

JJ Cookie-Base Blend	
Small	**Large**
1 1/2 Cups Sweet Rice Flour	3 Cups Sweet Rice Flour
1 Cup Rice Flour	2 Cups Rice Flour
3/4 Cup Potato Starch	1 1/2 Cups Potato Starch
1/2 Cup Tapioca Starch	1 Cup Tapioca Starch

This is a simple "lunch" menu example that can be used to select lunches and help track food inventory for planning.

Lunch Box	Out?	Child #1					Child #2				
		Mon	Tues	Wed	Thu	Fri	Mon	Tues	Wed	Thu	Fri
Main Item:											
Chicken Nuggets	x										
Turkey Hot Pocket											
Treats and Snacks											
Chocolate Chip Cookies	x										
Peanut Butter Brownie Cups											
Drinks											
Rice Milk											
Mango Juice											

Print this out, fold it in half, and keep it in your wallet. This quick card contains common items and is not a complete list. I've found it to be very helpful when grocery shopping.

Quick Gluten-Free Guidelines	Quick Casein-Free Guidelines	Quick Soy-Free Guidelines
Wheat free does *not* mean gluten-free.	Dairy-free does *not* mean casein-free.	Vegetable or plant protein are usually soy based.
Grains allowed: rice, corn (maize), potato, tapioca, gar-fava, sorghum, quinoa, millet, buckwheat, arrowroot, amaranth, teff, Montina, nut flours, and flax	Casein-free alternatives: rice, coconut, hemp, or potato-based milk, ghee butter with casein-free guarantee on label. Certified kosher or pareve.	Soy-free alternatives: Earth Balance soy-free margarine, Daiya cheese, Spectrum shortening, caramel syrup, molasses. See the Asian recipes in the book.
Grains *not* allowed: all wheat (einkorn, durum, faro, graham, kamut, semolina, spelt), rye, barley, and triticale.	Casein food *not* allowed: milk or milk chocolate, cream any kind, yogurt, sour cream, cheese, butter, ice cream, creamy soups, soup bases, puddings, custard, whey. Avoid ingredient with casein or caseinate.	Soy food *not* allowed: bean curd or tofu, bean sprouts, edamame, soy lecithin, Chinese black beans, miso, natto, soy nuts, soy protein, MSG, mono-glycirides and di-glycirides, soybeans or vegetable oil and shortening, textured vegetable protein (TVP), natural flavoring, teriyaki sauce.
May contain hidden gluten: beers, barley malt, dressing, energy bars, flavored oil, imitation bacon and seafood, natural flavor, modified food starch, nutritional supplements, processed meat, sauces and gravies, soup base.	May contain hidden casein: margarine, ghee butter, tuna fish, most dairy-free cheeses, lactic acid, artificial flavoring, chocolate bars, processed meat, cosmetics, and medicines.	May contain soy: Most Asian cuisines, chocolate chips, dressing, guar gum, lecithin, infant formula, natural flavoring, hydrolyzed plant or vegetable protein (HPP, HVP), thickener, gum, vegetable shortening or oil, stabilizer, vitamin E, mayonnaise, margarine, meat fillers for meat products, peanut butter, protein powders, sauces, gravies, soups or stock, smoothies.
Not on the list? Verify first.	Not on the list? Verify first.	Not on the list? Verify first.